Interwoven nature
relatedness and identity
in a changeful world

John Danvers

Whitewick Press

Copyright © 2016 John Danvers

Whitewick Press

All rights reserved

ISBN: 0995678901
ISBN-13: 9780995678903

For Philippa and our lovely family

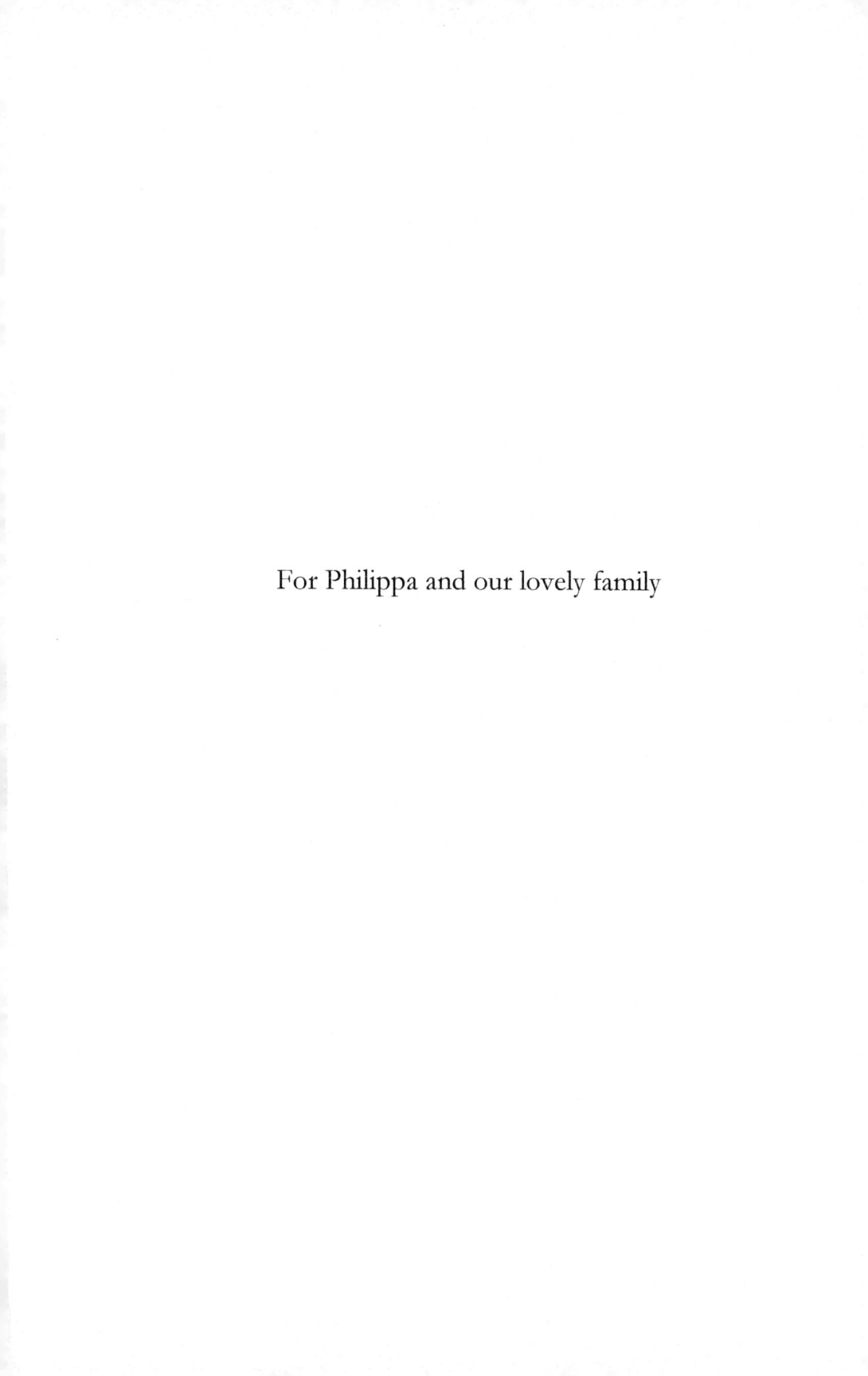

Acknowledgements

Thanks to Philippa and Jenny, Joanna and Tom for editorial advice. Some passages in Chapter XIII are developments of material included in a previous book: Agents of uncertainty: mysticism, scepticism, Buddhism, art and poetry, Rodopi, 2012. I am grateful to the organisers of numerous conferences for giving me the opportunity to present and discuss many of the themes explored in the following pages. And thanks to fellow students and seekers for the endless stimulation of lively minds.

CONTENTS

	Preface – about the title	9
	Introduction and outline of chapters	11
I.	Imagine an old man	17
II.	The permeable self	23
III.	How the old man sees things	41
IV.	Kith & kin – on being at home in the world	49
V.	The old man looks around	61
VI.	Intermingling minds	67
VII.	The old man remembers & ponders	81
VIII.	Buddhism, Daoism, Shamanism & nature	91
IX.	The old man observes the city	109
X.	The art of everyday living	115
XI.	The old man has dreams & nightmares	129
XII.	Being here – this world *is* heaven	135
XIII.	The old man sits on the balcony	151
XIV.	Revision & reorientation	159
XV.	The old man sees death as part of life	169
	Coda	177
	Bibliography	183

ILLUSTRATIONS

All drawings and photographs by the author, except pages 180-181.

Page

8	Handleaf
10	Two men
16	Old man
19	City Mist
22	Moving figure
28	Mycelium drawing
38	Lichen
40	Old shed study
43	Raven study
46	Woodland
48	Wall pictographs
55	Palaeo study
60	Face with spider
64	Every vagrant
66	Browning on stairs
76	Strandentwining memory
78	Estuary birds
80	Up the ridge
88	Cells and microbes
90	Monk mirror
96	Interwoven study
103	Head study
108	Frosty web
112	Window cranes
114	Kitchen window
119	The sensory field
124	Garden
128	Fire site
132	Fossil wasp study
134	Bird footprint
139	Relational field
142	Nama rupa

144	Tree study
150	City spires
153	Penumbra of uncertainty
156	Heron
158	Pond trees
164	Monk study
166	Magnolia
168	Interlacing trails
171	Dandelion seedheads
173	River
176	Face with lichen
180	Lindisfarne fragment
180	Islamic patterns
181	Polynesian patterns

Illustrations on pages 8-176 © John Danvers.

P. 180. Credit: Patricia Lovett. Online at: http://www.patricialovett.com/tag/lindisfarne-gospels/ Accessed 24/08/2016.

P. 180 (below). Credit: Wade Photo Archive. Online at: http://patterninislamicart.com/ Accessed 24/08/2016.

P. 181. Credit: West of Moon East of Sun Blog – photo of ceiling display in Metropolitan Museum of Art, New York. Online at: http://westofmooneastofsun.com/metropolitan-museum-of-art/ Accessed 24/08/2016

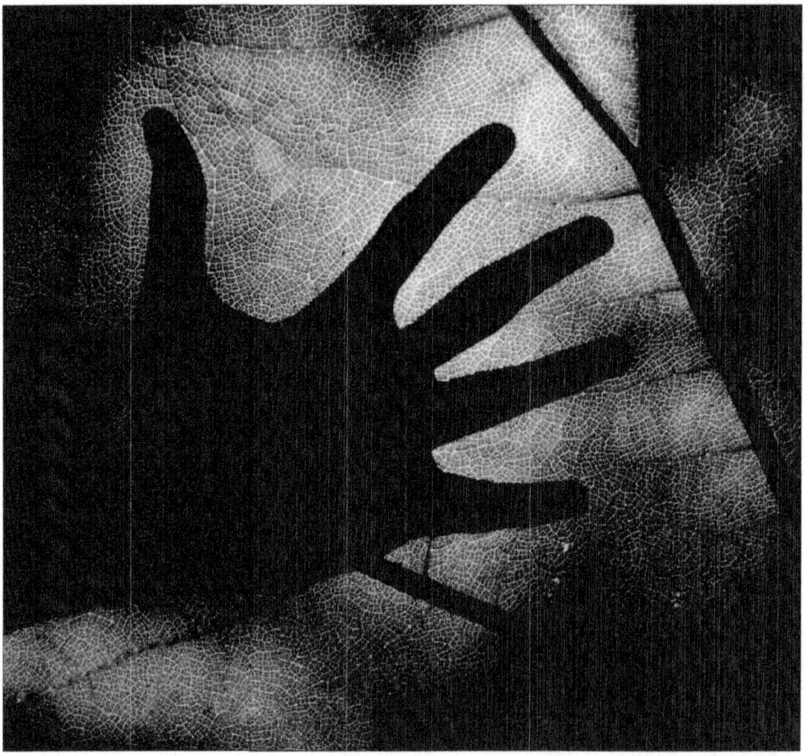

PREFACE - ABOUT THE TITLE

The main title, *Interwoven Nature*, suggests first, that we are ourselves, weavers and connectors. It seems to be in our nature to gather and weave, to use symbols, images and sounds to link together all manner of things, ideas, beliefs and intentions. We weave narratives of many kinds in order to plan, reflect and imagine. Literature and the arts, mathematics and the sciences, can be considered as highly-elaborate ways of relating one thing to another, in order to understand and celebrate the universe in which we live. Secondly, the title suggests that we are woven into nature, that we are participants in the natural world, implicated in it, rather than outsiders observing it from a distance. We are inextricably involved in what goes on around us. We are woven into the warp and weft of existence – even if we delude ourselves into thinking that we are somehow different from, or even superior to, the rest of creation. Thirdly, the title points to the fact that all of nature is interwoven into one coherent and seamless whole – the interconnected threads of life are woven into the fabric of the earth, its waters and skies. The universe is a dynamic interactive relational field, in which all entities, large and small, organic and inorganic, are bound together in a complex, noisy bustle of competitive interdependence and selfish co-operation – an infinite array of chemical, genetic and cultural forms giving rise to a hubbub of messages and stories.

The subtitle indicates that awareness of the interrelatedness of everything - together with the knowledge that we live in a world of endless change and impermanence - have profound implications for our own sense of identity, and for how we locate ourselves in, and navigate ways through, this fluid relational world – a world full of surprises, dangers, challenges and delights.

10   Interwoven Nature

INTRODUCTION AND OUTLINE OF CHAPTERS

In what follows there are two principal voices: an old man, who reflects on his life and offers us what small insights he has gained into the ways of the world; and a younger voice, more academic, sober and analytical. The former speaks in an enigmatic, allusive and, at times, rather naive register – he often misquotes from old texts and stumbles into poetry; the latter is prone to more abstract speculation with a tendency to gather, and comment on, readings of many authors. Both voices, and the personae they embody and articulate, are concerned with exploring their relationship with the world, particularly the natural world, and with trying to reach an understanding of how best to think of themselves as creatures *in*, and *of*, the world, rather than as outsiders observing the natural world as if it was an alien realm from which they are separated and removed.

In trying to convey a sense of connectedness and participation both voices articulate a view of humans as porous beings, flowing with an ever-changing stream of sensations, ideas, stories, images and signs. Viewed in this way each one of us is a confluence of countless currents of information and narrative - chemical, biological and cultural. These streams of information include: sensory coding passed from tongue to tongue, finger to finger, nose to nose, eye to eye; genetic coding passed from generation to generation; cultural coding passed from being to being and organism to organism. These trajectories of being, sensing and understanding cut across the apparent boundaries between species, pointing to a more cooperative and interactive state of existence, a world of shared inheritance, experience and reciprocal behaviours.

What follows can also be considered as a meditation on human identity and on our place in nature. Bringing together ideas drawn from ecology, science, Buddhism, Daoism, art, poetry and philosophy, with strands of poetic observation and fictional creation, I suggest that the natural world is a site of revelation, insight, grace and wonder – a place in which human beings can come to a realisation of who they are and how they are implicated in the world around them. The drawings and photographs are intended as a complementary narrative thread, adding a visual dimension to what is a multi-layered and multi-disciplinary enquiry into what it is to be here, privileged residents of a living planet in the midst of a universe about which we know so little.

As a counterpoint to the text the illustrations offer alternative perspectives on the main themes. Drawings and photographs by the author present structures and forms observed in the natural world – details of surfaces, shadows and things that convey something of the intricacy and beauty to be found in walks through the landscape. There are also images constructed out of superimposed and stitched-together fragments that evoke the way in which we relate to natural forms – how we weave interpretations and narratives around the endlessly varied structures of organism, stone, earth and water.

Many of the chapters are short and much of the text is structured in a collage form – parts stitched together in a way that echoes the overall theme of interweaving. This interwoven structure of ideas, examples, arguments and discussions is intended to be exploratory and provisional, rather than definitive and terminal - provocative and evocative rather than categorical and absolute. The somewhat unusual structure of the book arises from the multi-disciplinary nature of my research, and my background as an artist, writer and academic. It is an attempt to weave together scientific enquiry and analysis with poetic evocation and synthesis – a bringing together of evidence and intuition in the service of transforming our view of who we are and how we are in the world.

I hope the collage structure will help draw you, the reader, into thinking about yourself and the world in new ways – opening up a sense of exploration and curiosity about what it is to be a human being in a world of countless beings.

In chapter I, the old man is introduced. He talks about himself and where he lives – how his life is intertwined with his locality, a place that is part of him and he a part of it. For the old man there are no easily defined boundaries to himself or to his environment.

Chapter II is an essay about the self as a permeable and fluid process, a meeting place, a site of interaction, sensation, cognition and wonder. The fluidity and permeability of the self is considered with reference to atomic and cellular structures which are also seen to be dynamic and porous. The human body is also considered as a site inhabited by a community of organisms – the human being as a plurality of beings.

In chapter III, the old man remembers, or imagines, episodes in his long life - meetings and readings that have had a profound effect on how he sees the world and how he thinks about himself. He ponders on what others see as his solitary existence and what he considers to be his life of relationship with all the creatures around him.

This is followed, in chapter IV, by an essay about kinship and community, and about language and culture as agents of identity and relationship. Examples of poetry are used to show how nature comprises a polyphony of voices - a sacred music of vibrant interconnectedness.

In chapter V we return to the old man as he describes moments of quiet observation of animal life and reflects on the majesty of even the most mundane and marginal of living things.

Chapter VI explores the image of Venice as a metaphor for how communities and individuals consist of a confluence of thoughts, feelings and narratives – a site of interaction and exchange that establishes identity. This metaphor also underpins a discussion of the mind as a permeable structure that is also a confluence of influences, excitements, thoughts and feelings – a cosmopolitan place without clear boundaries, full of the comings and goings that constitute the mental locality of each person.

In the next chapter, VII, the old man looks back to his childhood and to the place where he grew up. He remembers his walks on the heathland behind his house, the family garden where his father grew flowers and vegetables and this sparks memories of two animal deaths in the wooded part of his own garden.

Chapter VIII is an essay about Buddhism, Daoism, shamanism and the processes of self-construction that make us who we are. These themes are explored in order to shed light on our relationship with the natural world – a relational field of interacting beings, processes and narratives.

In chapter IX the old man seems to be dreaming or imagining. He reflects on the pain and confusion in the world and how we deal with the changing nature of reality.

The essay that forms chapter X is about creativity and the craft of daily living. Contrasting views of creativity are discussed in relation to how we live in the world and how we act towards, and think about, our environment.

Chapter XI begins with the old man envisioning a bleak future of environmental depletion and degradation. He ponders on the remorseless passage of time and recites, to himself, a prayer that is a list of animals that have become scarce and needful of special protection.

Chapter XII is a brief essay about re-thinking the way in which we consider ourselves in relation to the earth upon, and within, which we live. The Buddhist term, *pratītyasamutpāda*, 'dependent origination', is explained, discussed and used to consider the causal nature of existence and the interdependence and interpenetration of all phenomena. The essay then returns to the theme of the porousness of human being.

In chapter XIII the old man recounts his experiences of practicing mindful meditation as a young man and how closely this way of being and observing echoed his childhood pastime of bird and animal watching.

The penultimate chapter, XIV, is devoted to a closer consideration of the Buddhist practice of mindful meditation and how this enables the practitioner to gain insight into, and come to terms with, two characteristics of existence: impermanence and interdependence.

In the final chapter the old man reflects on his own mortality and on the continuum of life, death and new life. He sees his own transient nature as a process interwoven into the transient nature of all of existence, and takes comfort from this recognition. He feels reassured and at peace knowing that he is making his own unique contribution to the playful interactive dance of atoms, cells, microbes and minds – and that we are all shape-shifting wanderers in an ever-changing universe.

A Coda follows gathering together some of the themes of the book and describing how the diverse forms of life on earth interact within networks of mutuality and cooperation. Our planet is circumscribed by innumerable sensory and information-processing systems – a vibrant web of signs, codes, stories and songs that weave together the lives of all the inhabitants of our earthly home.

16 Interwoven Nature

I. IMAGINE AN OLD MAN

*Then the friendless man wakes once more
and sees before him the dark waves, the
sea-birds on the waters spreading their wings,
frost and snow falling, mingled with hail.*[1]

I am not sure whether I have a skin anymore, or if I have it hardly seems to contain me. It has no definite surface that marks the boundary of my corporeal estate. It seems translucent and porous. I don't know where I end and the world begins. Sensations happen, they multiply like flocking birds skirling in the bright air. There is no steady centre to my being, as if I was dispersed over the whole field of my care and attention. I feel the pulse of this patch of earth like my own. There is nothing that seems outside or beyond, only a fluttering of sights and sounds and fragrances and the strange textures of substances that come and go as I pass through the rooms and open spaces of my home.

I seem to inhabit every nook and cranny of this place, a place that still delights and surprises me. I'm not alone here, though I rarely see anyone these days. I've got to know my fellow inhabitants and passers-by: roe deer coming up from the valley beyond to feed on early tender bluebells and late tasty dahlia flowers; badgers and foxes – generations of them; bats living in the tall dead totem of sweet chestnut that still rises from the heart of its new growth; wood mice with their big bright eyes; broods of slow worms and grass snakes raised in the heavy wooden compost bins; shoals of newts in the pond; frogs and toads, rare these days; saucy dragonflies and their dark armoured larvae; great spotted woodpeckers – always in pairs; garden warblers, dunnocks, tits of various kinds, braggardly magpies, shy jays, sweet-voiced blackbirds, cocky robins.... and the visiting ravens and crows and high-born buzzards and gulls and peregrines; and all the small creatures buzzing and hopping, scurrying, darting, flicking, sliding... leaving trails of sound, sight and smell in the air and on every surface; tall brittle turkey oaks, English oaks, elms that never get tall but always keep trying to, ashes peppering the soil with sleek grey seedlings, hazel and field maple and hawthorn and sloe; a cosmopolitan gathering of flowers, herbs and other plants for eating; fungi of many kinds sending out inquisitive tentacles to every root of every tree and shrub; and of course the ancient lichens and mosses minding their own business on walls and in hollows. Some of these residents and visitors I know by name but most I know without the hindrance of nomenclature. I know them for what they are and what they do and how they behave towards each other.

I am an old man. I've had a long life. No doubt about it – though there's doubt about most things. Maybe it's been more than one life. It feels like it. I've been here, in this house, for the past fifty years or so, other places before that. My memories of some of those places have grown faint and threadbare and I can only tell you what the weather was like or the view out of the window or what someone said as they leant against the doorframe.

But it's this house and its surroundings that I want to show you, with all its books, drawings, garden, and memories – some as stiff as my fingers, some as fresh and fluid as a mountain rill. If you come here some day, long after I seem to have gone, you might see over in that corner, by the door, a flicker of light as if the sun shone through a piece of fine vellum, or on that wall you might glimpse what look like the shadows of leaves, though there are no trees in the right place to cast such stains of dark. Sometimes you might feel a faint breeze on a still summer's day that catches at the skirts of tattered curtains and makes them dance. Occasionally you might hear the cackling of a green woodpecker rising eerily from the small dark wood only a stone's throw from the back door. I too have seen, heard and felt these things.

I'm so old I don't know whether my memories are memories or whether they're imaginings - stories conjured up to fill the holes and silences of forgetfulness. Who can tell?

I've been to many places, travelled here and there, seen a lot, yet seen little. So many places and stories only half-remembered, yet I can still smell the puddles and hear the closing of doors and the voices and the turning of pages – passing moments of crystalline detail.

I'll try to bring them to mind, dredge them out of the waters - silted, wet and dripping.

The old wooden house stands halfway up its narrow plot, besieged by ivy and half-strangled by a wisteria that was once a filigree of green and purple along its southern veranda but which now climbs all over the walls and roof. And the yew, dark and remote, still visited by generations of goldcrests, tiny flecks of colour amidst the shadows. Long ago, in the early years of the twentieth century, someone planted Monterey pines along the eastern boundary. They've grown tall, straight trunked, heavily built, with big limbs curving upwards at the tips. Back on the coast of central California, where they're native, the last few stands are struggling to survive, besieged by a fungal disease carried by bark beetles from tree to tree. Here they look dark on grey days but glow with a golden light on sunny evenings. On hot summer days the limpid air is riven by the sharp loud crackle of cones bursting open. In their homeland the pines grow in places where sudden forest fires pass quickly through the low branches, burning off the resinous twigs and needles, generating enough heat to make the large cones open their clenched fists and scatter a multitude of seeds on the burnt forest floor, ensuring rapid regeneration as they grow fast in the first twenty years of life, hopefully getting established before the next big fire comes along.

From the dilapidated veranda I can look out over the city to the distant hills topped with dark forest, ribbed with hedges and meadows that catch the sunlight of an evening. Sometimes the city and its cathedral are wreathed in river mist out of which the many churches raise their praying spires to the sky. Sometimes sea mist tumbles in along the estuary, shrouding the valley in a grey blankness. There's often a humming carried waywardly in the soft air, a muttering of voices and cars, the music of the city, a drone of business, shopping and endless human chatter - above which the cries of gulls, rooks and an occasional raven call out for consideration. From my aerie I can see a lot and hear a lot, catch the tide of human affairs washing against the stones, flowing in and out, day after day, year after year. Maybe once, long ago, Roman soldiers, serving time at the hill station just half a mile from here, stood in this spot looking down to the city where they could find love and drink and good food – such a relief from the rations they ate most days as they kept a lookout for strangers wandering in from the hostile lands all around.

The city is Exeter and I rarely go there. To the ancient British it was known as Caerwysc. The Romans called it, Isca Dumnoniorum, meaning 'Isca, capital city of the Dumnonii'. The Dumnonii were the British tribe who inhabited a large stretch of the southwest England peninsula. Isca probably comes from, Eisca, *a British word meaning 'a river abounding in fish'. Old Hoskins believes this may have been the root of the word 'Exe', the river that gives its name to the city.*[2] *The fish are nameless, like me.*

The house seems to have rooted itself in the Devon earth, immersed itself in the balmy air, soaking up the dampness blown in from the Atlantic and the dry heat peeling off the land mass to the east. The red cedar walls of the house have long since taken on the silvery complexion that old age bestows on this most generous of timbers. The roof, which once had a covering of felt and bitumen, is now reduced to marine plywood, slightly buckled and worn, like the deck of a neglected sailing boat. It is now as silvered and papery as the walls, yet it still holds the rain and wind at bay. Under its sheltering spread I can sit amongst my books and ponder on the ways of the world. I keep coming back to the words of a wanderer written in the famous Exeter Book, kept like a holy relic in the cathedral library:

> *In this world everything perishes and falls*
> *and no man can become wise until he has*

felt the winter's share of the turning world.[3]

I have often thought about these words, crafted many ages ago. We all have to feel the winter's share, the rough edges of what gets dealt to us. I've been lucky. No violence, no hunger or lack of water. I've not had to up sticks and move house and town and country. I've never felt the deep enmity of those around me, nor have I felt hatred in my turn. But I've seen these forces at work in the lives of others, and I've felt something of their power in words read or spoken.

---

[1] From *The Wanderer* elegy in 'The Exeter Book', a collection of Anglo-Saxon poetry presented by the eleventh century Bishop Leofric to Exeter cathedral library. My version of the Michelle Blair translation.
[2] See W.G.Hoskins. 1960. Two Thousand Years in Exeter. London: Phillimore, p. 7.
[3] From *The Wanderer*. My version of the Michelle Blair translation.

every atom belonging to me   as good belongs to you

II. THE PERMEABLE SELF

> '…what I assume you shall assume,
> For every atom belonging to me as good belongs to you'.
> Walt Whitman, in *Song of Myself* [1]

Although I agree with a lot of what the old man has to say, he does seem to exaggerate here and there, and I'm not sure he's always a reliable witness or observer of what happens. I'm going to approach things in a different way. Having collected a lot of material and made many notes, I'll try to fit these together in a manner that makes sense without seeming to be too insistent or water-tight. I hope there will be room for you to make up your own mind and to make connections of your own. I want to suggest rather than cajole, and to avoid dogmatic assertions. So I've organised my notes as my thoughts are structured: as a series of short bursts of activity, one idea leading to another. I'm not constructing a reasoned, step-by-step argument, but rather an organic unfolding of observations, associations, images and references. This seems to me to be more consistent with how I think and how I experience life as a succession of events, surprises, unpredictable twists and turns. Somehow the whole seems to have a coherence which is not apparent in its many parts. In other words I'm hoping that there is space within what I write for the fragmentary discontinuities that are a vital component of how we live, speak and share our experiences.

To begin with I want to explore some of the ways in which our sense of selfhood may need to be revised in the light of the idea that there is no fixed essence to who we are and that there are no definite boundaries to our embodied minds. We are highly porous beings, sharing our being with countless other organisms. Our embodied minds are also permeable – processing information from all around us, making our own contribution to the flow of signs, images and linguistic constructions that permeate the world of living organisms.

In many spheres there is a growing recognition that our current ideas, beliefs and patterns of behaviour are unsustainable - grounded as they are in the false assumptions that the earth is here for *our* (human) benefit and that the riches of the earth are infinite and inexhaustible. Individuals in many fields have been arguing for some time that we have to find, or rather devise, ways of living that *are* sustainable. In other words we have to change what we do and how we think about what we do, if we are to preserve the complex and finely-balanced structures that sustain life on our planet. Implicit in this way of thinking is a recognition that if we are to develop sustainable modes of interacting with, and making use of, the world's material resources, we have to change the way we think about ourselves and develop more sustainable ways of being. We have to think of ourselves as beings *in*, and *of*, the world – as embodied fields of consciousness participating in an indeterminate flux of chemical, biological and cultural interactions.

In this chapter I'm going to explore some ideas about the ways in which human beings, as minded organisms, are implicated in the environment, an environment that is alive with other organisms, each of which is a manifestation of a particular culture - each culture characterised by particular ways of looking *out* at the world, while also participating *in* the world.

First, a historical digression. Since at least the 17th century in the West there has been, and perhaps there still is, a tendency to view the self and its relation to the world in what might be labelled Cartesian or Newtonian terms (though this over-simplifies the thinking of both René Descartes and Isaac Newton). The terms Newtonian-self or Cartesian-self have been used as short-hand for a set of ideas and values which are deeply dualistic and mechanistic. While Newton, argues for a model of the world as a clockwork machine-like system composed of distinct and solid bodies that interact according to deterministic processes and laws, Descartes emphasises the separateness of things and the importance of rational thought as a way of understanding the world, a form of understanding that is analytical and, supposedly, objective. Descartes believes that 'the mind is a non-physical substance'[2] wholly distinct from the physical body. This separation of mind and body, aligned with Christian dualisms such as, God/humanity, spirit/matter, heaven/earth, is one of the foundations of scientific and philosophical thinking in the West.

These ideas, combined with Descartes' famous statement, *'cogito ergo sum'* ('I am thinking, therefore I exist'), tend to privilege thought, rationality and reason, over feeling, irrationality and intuition. Philosophical and scientific enquiry is a process of constructing rational answers to rational questions. We can see from this how scientific objectivity, abstract thinking and human consciousness tends to be valued more highly than the arts, subjectivity, sensory perceptions and the realms of the non-human. Rational understanding becomes the focus of science – a process of systematically dividing, categorising and finding *reasons*. The use or exploitation of the physical world becomes the focus of technology – and the material world is seen as being separate from the human mind and from the divine realm of God.

As Margaret Midgley argues:

> The notion of our selves - our minds - as detached observers or colonists, separate from the physical world and therefore from each other, watching and exploiting a lifeless mechanism, has been with us since the dawn of modern science.[3]

From this perspective the earth and the natural world become a largely inanimate resource to be exploited for the benefit of mankind - a vast bank of materials to be converted into energy and goods for trade and use. As Midgley goes on to say:

> [This Cartesian approach] …produced a huge harvest of local knowledge… But it has made it very hard for people even to contemplate putting the parts together…[4]

In recent times systems theory, complexity theory, consciousness studies, hermeneutics, pragmatism and other strands of philosophy, and the whole field of ecology, demonstrate attempts to overcome Cartesian dualism and fragmentation - by looking at systems as interdependent, mutually interactive processes that have to be considered holistically - as wholes that amount to more than the sum of their parts.

*

We can look at these matters from another perspective. In the reductive search for the ultimate substance, which was once a goal for the so-called 'hard' sciences, the atom was posited as the building block out of which the universe was built – Democritus, the Greek, (c.460-c.370BC) was one of the first to believe this. But as the atom was mapped in the early part of the twentieth century, researchers realised that the atom itself was more like a cloud than a speck of dust, a cloud that was largely empty space – a tiny field of energy bounded by the shifting trajectories of electrons, neutrons, protons and other sub-atomic forces. In Bill Bryson's words, the atom-cloud is a 'zone of statistical probability marking the area beyond which the electron only very seldom strays'.[5] Bryson also reminds us that 'if an atom were expanded to the size of a cathedral, the nucleus [the zone of neutrons and protons] would be only about the size of a fly'.[6] It is this concrete emptiness which lies at the paradoxical heart of our solid world. The things we bump into, the hammer that hits the nail (or our thumb) and the chair we sit on, are quite literally condensations of space that happen to reflect, refract or transmit light, and thus be visible to one apparatus or another, including the human eye. The mystery as to how indeterminate minds can be at the same time congealed-jelly-like brains, is only slightly more puzzling than how clouds of sub-atomic forces in vast numbers of almost empty porous bubbles can be at the same time a turnip or a diamond.

The other paradoxical feature of atoms, hardly believable, is that despite their smallness and delicate cloud-like fuzziness, they are remarkably durable. It is almost certainly the case that every atom in my body, or yours, has passed through many stars and been part of millions of other organisms before becoming me or you and passing on to be part of countless other entities. In his inimitable way, Bryson points out that atoms are so numerous and so enduring, that any or all of us, may now be composed of billions of atoms that were once part of Shakespeare, or Buddha, or Hildegard of Bingen, or, spare the thought, any human embodiment of evil you care to imagine – though it takes, apparently a number of decades before atoms come thoroughly back into circulation after they have been embodied, so to speak.[7]

These characteristics of atoms and their sub-atomic constituents raise obvious questions about our own sense of self-ownership, self-identity and solidity. We are all atomic cousins and we need to be mindful of the long dead ancestors whose atoms we may share – constituent parts of this temporary atomic structure we call our body or our self. And we should keep in mind that atoms are utterly indifferent to the race or religion of the so-called individuals to whose lives they give form and temporary shelter. These intermingled atoms don't recognise bodily boundaries, national boundaries, political differences or any of the petty conflicts that arise from notions of purity, autonomy or exclusivity. The most fanatical ideas of ethnic and religious difference arise in brains that share a common and universal atomic ancestry. We are all atomic hybrids.

*

To take a different tack, Umberto Eco quotes Dionysius the Areopagite, who describes the beauty of the universe in which 'all things [are drawn] together in a state of mutual interpenetration'.[8] This echoes the thinking and experience of many Buddhist practitioners (see chapter VIII). It also resonates with comments made by Kenneth Rexroth in his long poem, The Dragon and the Unicorn, written in the late 1940s as he travelled through Europe in the shadow of World War II:

> Each moment of the universe
> And all the universes
> Are reflected in each other
> And in all their parts and
> Thence again in themselves.
> It is simpler to see this
> As a concourse of persons, all
> Reflecting and self-reflecting
> And the reflections and the
> Reflective medium reflecting.[9]

In a later poem entitled, They Say This Isn't a Poem, Rexroth writes: 'All being is contingent, / No being is self-subsistent'.[10]

*

Inside every apparently solid object there is an infinity of space, just as in every mind there is an imaginative infinity – though can we really speak of *a* mind (for where are its boundaries) and can a mind (which is an indeterminate field of energies, firing at great speed and unfathomable complexity) have an inside? Where is the boundary of my bodymind and how can I disentangle *my* thinking, sensing, hoping and believing from yours. Aren't we all more like a forest, a patch of brambles, or a confluence of trickles of rainwater merging into a stream, a river and a sea, or are we more like an intermingling of clouds.

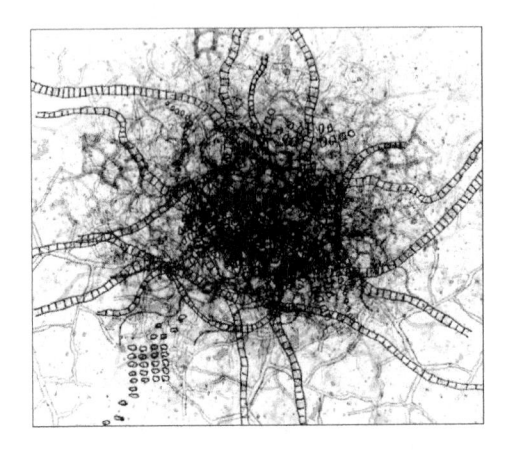

As a metaphor for this intermingling of minds and of chemical and biological processes it may be useful to think of the *mycelium* of a fungus: the mass of thread-like filaments that exist below the ground through which the fungus absorbs and processes nutrients. *Mycelia* often spread over large areas, interconnecting and interweaving with each other. They are dynamic chemical networks that help to maintain the well-being of many habitats – particularly woodlands, forests and temperate grasslands. The apparently *individual* mushroom or toadstool is only a part, the fruiting body, of a much larger and more indeterminate organism. Maybe *we* are only the fruiting bodies of networks of thoughts and signs, imaginations and constructions – networks that we refer to as cultures.

*

Writing from a Sufi perspective, Shaikh ad-Darqâwî notes, 'You are an illusion and a nothingness in a nothingness'. He goes on: 'if you were to examine yourself, you would find God instead of finding yourself, and there would be nothing left of you but a name without a form'.[11]

*

In our experience of things-in-the-world we seem to encounter volume, solidity, materiality, substance – yet the appearance of substance is deceptive when looked at through three different lenses. Firstly, through our perceptual experience we discover that the object is not a static stable entity but a dynamic part of a continually changing field of perceptual and interpretative activity. Secondly, through our cognitive processes, particularly scientific modes of enquiry, we encounter at the sub-atomic and quantum levels a world of interpenetrating energies and forces. Thirdly, in considering our existential condition we find our own identity or self to be anything but a fixed, finite, object-like construction – rather it is a matrix of at times contradictory moods, feelings, thoughts, processes which somehow cohere but are open to continual revision and transformation as we negotiate changing circumstances and conditions.

As Arthur Eddington points out: 'The external world of physics has thus become a world of shadows. In removing our illusions we have removed the substance, for indeed we have seen that substance is one of the greatest of our illusions'.[12]

It is interesting to note that the term used by the sceptics of ancient Greece to denote the indeterminacy of things, the lack of essence or self-existence, is *aoristia*, 'lack of boundary or definition'. This may be seen as corresponding quite closely to *sunyata* in the Madhyamika school of Buddhism. Thomas McEvilley points out that the indeterminacy of things makes them ungraspable in epistemological terms. Having no self-existence, things cannot be 'circumscribed by concepts' or defined or grasped by linguistic terms. This ungraspable, ineffableness is what the sceptics call *akatalepsia*. Hence the sceptics argue that we need to practice 'suspension of judgement' (*epoché*) & 'non-assertion' (*aphasia*).[13]

Some Buddhists refer to nature as Big Mind, an indeterminate field of interpenetrating beings and intelligences. Everything causes everything else – 'mutual co-arising'. And every entity (including our self) is a process, an event, a burst of information, sensation and experience illuminating Big Mind for a moment then melting away into a pool of history that becomes accessible and shared through a symbolic memory of stories, songs, poems, images, artefacts and dance.

*

Baruch Spinoza approaches ideas of mutuality and inter-relationship from a different perspective. In the *Ethics*, which was published just after he died in 1677, he argues for a new way of thinking about God, nature and human moral behaviour. He maintains that it is only the infinite everything, the universe as a whole, that is 'self-subsistent', the one infinite undifferentiated substance. Every *thing* can only be a part of that totality, a subsistent aspect of the whole, dependent for its existence on all the other parts of the whole. According to Quinton, Spinoza is only logically developing Descartes' definition of substance as, 'that which requires nothing but itself in order to exist'.[14] For the deeply religious Spinoza this meant that, in Quinton's words, 'the only true substance is God'. Therefore for Spinoza, the infinitude of God means there can be nothing outside of God, because if there were anything outside God it would follow that God had boundaries and was therefore finite – 'If God is infinite then God must be co-extensive with everything'.[15] Looked at from another perspective, if nature is the totality of what there is, then both God and Nature must be infinite and therefore they must be identical, one unitary substance. Note the similarity with Buddhist notions of mutuality of existence, and with ecology. In both, the universe is considered as a relational field, rather than as a field of separate things or essences.

If we are all manifestations of the mutuality of existence, participating in the interpenetration and interdependence of all things, including organisms with each other and with the environment, how does this impact upon the way we think about ourselves? Our human skin can be seen as both a porous zone through which we interact with everything that surrounds us, and as the skin of the world. There is a unity of inside and outside. At the chemical, micro-biological and quantum levels there are no easy and obvious distinctions between one organism and another, or between organism and environment, subject and object, observer and observed. We are all implicated in the whole of existence, participants in the web of being and becoming.

A vivid description of this interdependence is given by Lewis Thomas. He describes how, in the most intimate way, each of us provides, in each of our bodies, a habitat for other organisms.

> There they are, moving about in my cytoplasm... They are much less closely related to me than to each other and to the free-living bacteria out under the hill. They feel like strangers, but the thought comes that the same creatures, precisely the same, are out there in the cells of seagulls, and whales, and dune grass, and seaweed... and further inland in the leaves of the beech in my backyard, and in the family of skunks beneath the back fence, and even in that fly on the window.[16]

Given the ways in which organisms and ecosystems are woven into each other, how are we to refer to ourselves. When I say 'me' am I really referring to a whole community of organisms of which 'me' is the collective title? Am 'I' an assembly of immigrants, a place in which many organisms reside? How can I call this body 'mine' when it is a gathering-place of creatures, all of whom are tenants, residents, citizens? Aren't 'my' thoughts and feelings as much 'theirs'? Is the consciousness that arises in this body a collective consciousness? Whose is this mind I treat as if it were mine? Shouldn't the term 'I' be replaced by 'we' and 'mine' by 'ours'?

*

Let us consider the implications of these observations about the intermingling of entities and beings, and relate them to ideas about self, identity and subjectivity drawn from the German philosopher, Martin Heidegger. Given that what we like to call *our* bodies provide a home for a host of organisms, an open-house if you like, we can also think of the self as an open-work, a work in progress, an ever-changing process of interaction between a community of organisms and the environment. There is no fixed essence to this self as there is no unchanging bio-chemical essence to the human body. At one point in his book, *Irrational Man*, William Barrett is discussing Heidegger. He writes:

> My being is not something that takes place inside my skin (or inside an immaterial substance inside that skin); my Being, rather, is spread over a field or region which is the world of its care and concern. Heidegger's theory of man (and of Being) might be called the Field Theory of Man (or the Field Theory of Being) in analogy with Einstein's Field Theory of Matter, provided that we take this purely as an analogy.[17]

In Heidegger's view human existence involves being-in-the-world, an active field of being that Heidegger calls *Dasein*. As Barrett points out, we can think of this like a magnetic field, yet without a solid magnet at its centre. We are implicated in the world whether we like it or not. We care about it and are concerned with it, whether we live in an urban high-rise or a cottage in deepest Devon. We are dependent on the earth for food, water, heat, light, the materials out of which we build our lives and our artefacts, and for the aesthetic nourishment that nature provides. Through our senses, our breathing, eating and drinking we absorb and converge with the world around us – there is a fundamental permeability to our being-in-the-world. Our being involves reciprocity with a dynamic, ever-changing, ambient space that gives form and meaning to us as we give form and meaning to it. *Dasein* means to be there – or perhaps, to be *here*. In Barrett's words:

> Man does not look out upon an external world through windows, from the isolation of his ego: he is already out-of-doors. He is in the world because, existing, he is involved in it totally.[18]

It is interesting to note that Heidegger also uses a forest metaphor to describe *Dasein* as an opening or clearing in which possibilities arise – human *being* is, paradoxically, an absence, an open indeterminate space in which things become present. We can extend this aspect of Heidegger's thinking to describe human beings as agents of consciousness in the world, the world being conscious through us. Each of us presents a distinctive worldview in so far as we are located at different points within the wider field, yet we offer shared perspectives in so far as our fields of being conjoin, inter-flow and eddy around each other – as currents do in a stream or river.

It is important to remember that we share our presence in the world with others. Our being, our field of concern, overlaps with, and interpenetrates, other fields of being and concern. We are inextricably interwoven into the fabric of existence. The boundaries of bodies and minds, organisms and habitats, are porous and fluid, determined more by convention and the needs of human language, than by any actual fixity of division. Filaments of consciousness and self are intertwined, forming the multi-dimensional mycelia of cultures.

*

Guy Davenport suggests that,

> The imagination... [is] rooted in a ground, a geography. The Latin word for the sacredness of a space is *cultus*, the dwelling of a god, the place where a rite is valid. *Cultus* becomes our word *culture*, not in the portentous sense it now has, but in a much humbler sense. For ancient people the sacred was the vernacular ordinariness of things: the hearth, primarily; the bed, the wall around the yard.[19]

Davenport points to the paradox that cultures, matrices of evolving minds and avenues of exchange, like each entity or self, are both located in a place and yet indeterminate. They are somewhere, as we are in this room, yet, at the same time, they are everywhere, in the sense that our minds or imaginations have no obvious boundaries – just as a chair is both a substantial *thing* and a cloudy bundle of sub-atomic particles in a constant state of flux.

*

Let us briefly consider the relationship between mind and the world from another point of view. A mind may be centred in a body but it is not contained or defined by it. Mind may be embodied while not being co-extensive with a body – it extends into the world and into other minds. In this sense it is boundless and non-spatial. Through many forms of language and symbolic systems many minds are interwoven into a culture or many cultures. It is hard to imagine how language and ideas could arise in a single bounded mind. Somehow minds have to open out, reach for, and interact with, other minds – to extend into the world beyond the immediate, apparent boundary of a particular physical body.

Of course, our bodies can be extended by the use of material aids - such as a toothbrush, a hammer, spectacles, a blind person's stick, a bicycle or a car – enabling us to perceive more clearly, to overcome a limitation or to move more swiftly. In a similar way our minds can be extended by the use of a notebook, counting on our fingers, and by using mobile phones and computers – enabling us to undertake mental tasks more quickly and accurately. Novels, paintings and other artworks can be considered as extensions of our minds - repositories and agents of memory, imagination, ideas and images. These extensions also enable us to share experiences, communicate with others, learn from the past and plan for the future. All of these devices extend the reach and scope of our embodied minds beyond the apparent borders of our skin, skull, brain and senses.

These notions of bodily and mental extension, and the intermingling of minds, can be linked to the theories of extended cognition and mind first put forward by Andy Clark and David J. Chalmers in 1998. In their paper, The Extended Mind, they argue that cognitive processes 'aren't all in the head' – giving the example of language as 'one of the central means by which cognitive processes are extended into the world.' They go on to pose the question, 'does the spread of cognitive processes out into the world imply some correlative leakage of the self into local surroundings?' And they answer: 'It seems so. Most of us already accept that the boundaries of the self outstrip the boundaries of consciousness: My dispositional beliefs, for example, constitute in some deep sense part of who I am. If so, then our [....] boundaries may also fall beyond the skin.' They conclude their paper with the following words: 'once the hegemony of skin and skull is usurped, we may be able to see ourselves more truly as creatures *of* the world.'[20]

One consequence of the coming together of these strands of thought is the realisation that incompleteness, instability and openness are characteristics of the self-as-open-work. The self as process, rather than as object, is in continuous construction. We weave and compose as we are woven and composed. There is no end to self-construction except in death, and even then we might consider the finite ego-self as being dissolved into, or reformed as, another kind of construction which is the network of objects and stories we have made in the world, and the memories and stories associated with us that are made in the minds of others. In this sense our artefacts and stories, our bodymind, are continued, revised and absorbed into the collective stories of a culture, into the unfolding communal mind.[21]

*

The poet, Gary Snyder, reminds us that mountains and waters are bound together as two interpenetrating and interdependent vectors of geography and myth.[22] Walking in the mountains, fording streams, being enveloped in clouds on rocky paths, is to activate and realise the mythic structures that are immanent in the landscape. Knowledge is transmitted from age to age through the symbolic codes embedded in the cultural ecology of each place. Mind and mountains, poetry and waters, myths and land are inseparable and mutually reinforcing. The landscape, with all its constituent energies and beings, is alive with inherited knowledge, passed along lines of culture from microbe to microbe, plant to plant, animal to animal, human to human. As we walk in the landscape, biological and cultural evolutionary realms are fused in narratives of stone, water, fibre, air and light. Each strand of the ecological web sings its songs, tell its tales, inscribes its drawings, and all are orchestrated in a great improvisatory *gesamkunstwerk* that is forever evolving in an ocean of indeterminacy.

*

We can conceive of the artist/poet as a nomad, as a walker and wanderer, and as a hunter-gatherer, gathering together in one place-object-text the fruits of the forest. The forest being both the locus and life of the poet – experiences, perceptions, feelings, imaginings and dreams – and the layered histories, narratives and cultures of other forest-dwellers – the common-wealth of beings for whom the poet acts as consciousness, voice, scribe, mythmaker and imagemaker.

*

We are thinking bones, muscles of imagination in a field of light. We show and speak ourselves in many different ways, yet all are variations, reiterations, reworkings and reshowings of themes, patterns and structures that are recognisably of this bodymind, this locus of becoming, knowing and doing – this many-roomed house of bone and light. We don't live *in* this bonehouse, we *are* this mobile bonehome – this is how we are minded, fitted to the world, nomadic residents of each site of being.

And there are many openings into the skin-and-bone-house. Many gaps and fine-meshed curtains through which breezes skitter, light pours in (and out), and waves of sound set sensitive membranes vibrating. And the mind is similarly configured - a web of light in which the past is made present and the future arises in every moment.

>   so many openings
>   through which the world
>   enters,
>   mingles,
>   melts into me
>
>   only to flow on
>   into others, world
>   into self, self into
>   world,
>
>   like sticks in a stream,
>   bent by the light, we
>   pass through a prism
>
>   rainbowed and scattered
>   we are not what we
>   seem

All things are permeable and in flux. We are all endlessly exchanging energies with everything that is around us. We are transparent vessels through which pass waves of sound, cosmic radiation and light. There is no clear boundary between inside and outside. But most of the time we think and act as if there is. Art and poetry can open up the realm of interrelatedness and indivisibility through the use of metaphor, analogy, imagination and association - reconnecting the invisible strands of relationship that have been broken by institutional languages and signs.

*

'To sustain' carries both the sense of enduring, keeping going, carrying on, and the sense of giving nourishment to, supporting or holding. In all these senses cultural diversity across all life forms is as important as bio-diversity and chemical diversity. The arts, like the sciences, can help us to gain a more durable, sustainable understanding and kinship, grounded (or *skied* or *watered*) in a multi-perspectival view, a gathering of learnings from all quarters, from many minds, many bodies, many modes of being.

The term 'sustainability' also implies that the use of resources 'is conducted in a manner that protects the resource base for use by future generations'.[23] An important part of that 'resource base' is the polyphony of cultures and languages, human and non-human, which speaks to us *of* ourselves and *about* the world we inhabit. Sustaining this polyphony, the cultural music of fibre, flesh and bone, is a necessity if our view of ourselves is rooted in a deep sense of kinship and mutuality with all forms of existence. It is this self-orientation that enables us to look both to our feet and to the horizon, to combine a buzzard's eye view with a worm's touch, to re-vision ourselves as porous and permeable, in interdependent co-relation with all entities, sensitive to the polyphony of the many, rather than to the monologue of the one.

Maybe in this way we can extend our appreciation of the human arts to include the arts and cultures of animals and birds, trees and fish – to be sustained by, and to help sustain, both the swallow's pirouetting flight and the slow movement of the lichen that grows millimetre by millimetre over hundreds of years on a rough patch of Dartmoor stone.

---

[1] Walt Whitman, *Song of Myself*, in Leaves of Grass, 1947: 23
[2] in Anon 2000: 217
[3] Midgley 2001: 19
[4] *ibid*: 20
[5] Bryson 2004: 189
[6] *ibid*: 184
[7] *ibid*: 176
[8] Eco 2002: 18
[9] Rexroth 2003: 337
[10] *ibid*: 598
[11] in Baker & Henry 1999: 172 – my version in modern English
[12] in Anon. 2002: 128
[13] McEvilley 2002: 458
[14] in Magee 1987: 101
[15] *ibid*: 102
[16] in Capra 1990: 294
[17] Barrett 1990: 217
[18] *ibid*: 217
[19] Davenport 1984: 4
[20] Clark & Chalmers 1998
[21] Danvers 2006: 157
[22] Snyder 2004: 8-10
[23] Bullock and Trombley 2000: 849

40   Interwoven Nature

III. HOW THE OLD MAN SEES THINGS

My house has many rooms and in one of them, a small almost square space with a large window facing south, I often sit to write and draw. Over the window a blind hangs down to keep out the bright sunlight. It turns the garden outside into a tableau of ghostly forms, always dimly visible yet never seen. Here I sit and write, referring to myself as another, as an everyman:

> *In the darkness or gazing out*
> *from a cobwebbed window,*
> *what he saw sometimes*
> *left him mute, silenced by*
> *shadows, untongued by*
> *a despair that was also*
> *joy*
>
> *amongst dirt & decay*
> *a new identity came to be*
> *scribbled in him by woodlice,*
> *spiders & snails*
>
>   *this was*
> *where he stood, neglected*
> *by lucidity,*
>   *half in & half*
> *out of the light*

On the wooden floor, stained by years of splashed paint and drops of ink, a sheet of paper becomes a world of possibility. On it I draw, marking out the days with my brush. Each dying moment is entombed in a stain on the paper, a line for each movement of my mind, arm and wrist. Day after day, year after year, my life unfolds in a trail of marks. Here I write and draw and don't know why.

There is no greater magic than conjuring form out of void, minding the unminded, pulling into the light of day what had been only a wisp of possibility.

One, two, three, four, five........ I remember meeting a young girl on a hillside counting daisy heads. It was summer. The air was still. Every now and again she looked up at the sky and watched a cloud or a lazy bird drifting by. After a few minutes she turned back to the daisies and began to count all over again. One, two, three, four, five, six, seven....... She never got further than one hundred. For her there were only one hundred daisies on the hillside, while for me, there were countless thousands.

Habitus. Habitat. Hermitage. Palace. Castle. House. Hut. Hovel. Bivouac. Shelter. Cabin. Shack. Cave. There's not much difference. A place to sit and rest, to dry out, eat and make love. A place to chew the cud and ponder. Big, small, grand, humble – they all fall down in the end.

I remember Basho's words:

> *This grassy hermitage*
> *no more than five feet*
> *square, I'd gladly leave*
> *but for the rain.[1]*

Some days the world seems up close, tight against my skin. Each sensation plunges deep. In one of my dreams I'm pushing through a bramble patch. Arcs of thorn grab at me. My skin stammers in pain and delight. I eat the wild honey. Taste stones and pine juice. Lick heartwood. Smell the wings of powdery moths. Drink rain cupped in hollows where spiders weave their histories: generations of silken dwellings tufted with dust and faint luminescence, moonlight caught on each fibre. There are so many sunsets to see, hours of darkness to feel, stars to wonder at.

> *Shivering in the rain*
> *stammering in the*
> *moonlight*

How the old man sees things   43

*there is no end
to what can
turn our words
inside out
upside down
jibjibbering
at the glory
of it all*

In my library - which spills out from the scribing and drawing space into other rooms, on to shelves sagging with the weight of words, piled here and there along corridors and on the occasional stair – I have many strange volumes, or at least their titles seem unusual to my rare visitors: The Book of Soil, The Book of Rain, The Book of Leaves, The Book of Ash, The Books of Lightning (one page to each book, who knows how many), The Book of Clouds, The Book of Beetles, The Book of Birds, The Book of Night, The Book of Evenings, The Book of Forgotten Things, The Book of Things Never Seen, The Book of Familiar Things, The Book of Underneath, The Book of Changing Light, The Book of Storms, The Book of Wings…. They're all bound in what looks like hand-made paper. The same hand has written the titles on the covers, never on the spine. It is my writing.

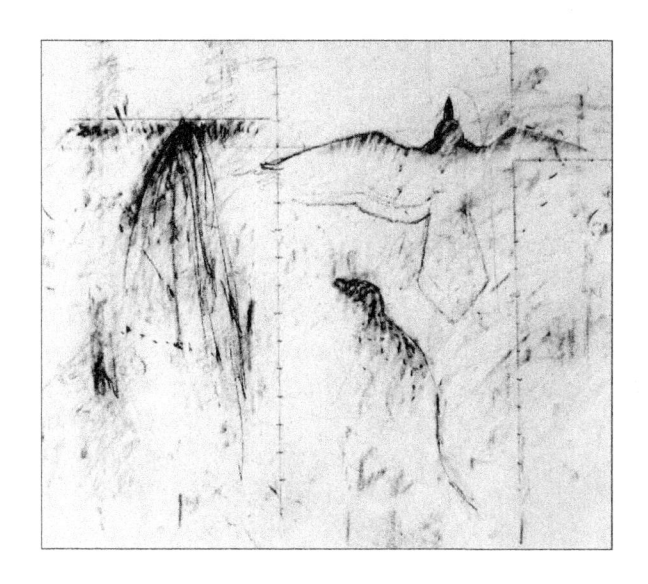

I have dreams of living on a coastal rockstack where gulls and ravens nest. It's an outpost of sea pink and guano fingering the sky, at its base turbulent waters scrabble at the red rock, polishing it until it glistens in the fleeting sunlight. The birds bring news of what humans are up to: the wars and petty rages; the clans and sects; the fashion for this or that; the torrents of words, images, messages; the craving for wealth and fame; the insistent drumming of the poor and hungry on the doors of the rich; the plans for equality and freedom endlessly revised, endlessly postponed.... It was all of this, in my dream, that I had sought to escape in my lofty retreat. But I knew there was no escape. I knew that all these troubles were as dogged as the waves nibbling at my feet. No matter what I did to run away they always found me out.

> *Exiled on the shivering sea, my brothers were the cackling gannets and whimpering petrels. All humanity were strangers who lived in the silver city where trees grew and laughter still had a place. As a homeless outlaw I left behind the dust of the world in order to tramp this bleached and fickle whale-road where God metes out hatred and compassion with equal indifference.*[2]

Some time ago I read a book about eccentric loners who set out on what is called, fuga mundi, *the flight from the world. In one section the author introduces us to a contemporary Northumberland hermit, Sister Maximilian, an ex-Benedictine nun. As a hermit, possessing nothing, the Sister argues that she is more able to feel solidarity with the poor. She can also more easily feel what it is like to count every penny to see if there is enough for a loaf of bread. She can feel closer to those who have no roof over their heads, and to those who have to sleep in the street. For it isn't that Sister Maximilian, and others like her, don't care for the world - quite the contrary. This is God's world and if you are in love with God, you are in love with this world. You are not rejecting it. By spending hours alone in prayer and contemplation, wearing away at the cravings, false needs and desires that fuel the troubles of the world, Sister Maximilian manifests another way of being in the world. Or at least that is what she hopes and believes.*[3]

At times I'm amused by the contrariness of it all. Like the good Sister I'm often called a hermit because I seem to live alone, up here on the hill, out of the city – although why anyone thinks I'm alone when I'm surrounded by so many fellow creatures. To most people hermits seem to live a strange life cut off from the world, separated from the hurly burly of life as it is lived by the majority. But that's not how I see it. To me it feels as if I am more closely in touch with things, open to all that happens in a way that I could never be if I was still living cheek by jowl with my kinfolk. To live in the city it is usually necessary to wear armour, to carry around a carapace of protection from the jostling crowd. In the city we have to wear a mask, to pretend we are so many different personae to so many different people. We act the part that best fits the situation. And we often say things and do things that we later regret or feel we shouldn't have done. We get carried along by all kinds of forces that drag us into arguments, set us against our neighbours, lead us into temptations of all kinds and leave us feeling shallow and confused. We also feel jealousy, anger and irritability. Somehow the world seems against us. We feel threatened and cut off from those around us. It's as if we no longer belong.

But surely this is what everyone says hermits are supposed to feel: cut off, separated from the community, isolated and remote! In reality, it's the other way around. To spend time alone, or in a community where solitude is respected and where contemplation is practiced as a great art, is to spend time reconnecting with the world and with the beings that inhabit our world. Most hermits are contemplatives and in contemplation we sew together what has been torn apart and we feel again the wonder of being-in-the-world and being-with-others. We take off our armour, put down our weapons and our masks, and stand once more in our own light, at one with the world. Or at least that's how I see it. I've met many hermits. Some of them live alone. Some live with their families. Some live in large communities. Being a hermit, in this sense is to be in *the world, not out of it.*

In my notes I find something I read many years ago. It was written by Nicholas the Frenchman, a hermit who lived on Mount Carmel in the early part of the thirteenth century. He is describing his own experiences living on the mountain:

> *Listen to what marvellous, unbelievable consolations we hermits receive both in mind & body. For in solitude all the elements protect us. The wonderful beauty of the sky, ornamented with the stars & planets, attracts us and raises us to things more sublime. The birds, like angels as they seem, sing their lovely melodies for our comfort. The mountains*

run with sweetness; the hills are full of milk & honey, but are never to be tasted by the foolish lovers of the world. The stems shoot up from the roots, the grass grows green, the shady trees refresh our eyes; the most beautiful flowers unfold & scent the air; and all is for us, the hermits. The silent sparkling stars speak to us in words of salvation. The shrubs with their luxurious foliage give us comfort, and all the creatures which we see & hear in our solitude refresh & strengthen us as if we were their brethren...[4]

[1] My version of a poem in Nobuyuki Yuasa's translation of *Narrow Road to the Deep North*, Penguin, 1966. P.104

[2] The old man seems to be half-remembering another narrative from The Exeter Book – *The Seafarer*. He gives us here a confused and bastardised version. Much condensed, it has a certain lively charm.

[3] Isabel Colegate, *A Pelican in the Wilderness: hermits, solitaries and recluses*, HarperCollins, 2002. P.233

[4] This may be from Anson, P.F. (1964): The Call of the Desert, S.P.C.K

48 Interwoven Nature

IV. KITH & KIN - ON BEING AT HOME IN THE WORLD

In the light of the old man's comments about connection and disconnection, let us consider in more detail the relationship between the individual and the community. First, a broad brush outline: in some ways the history of western thought from the seventeenth century (Descartes) to the twentieth (Wittgenstein) is a history of an increasing sense of alienation between human beings and the natural world. The world of mountains, valleys, birds and animals tends to be increasingly viewed as a world of organic and mineral substances to be used to satisfy more or less immediate human needs for food and shelter. Since the publication of Rachel Carson's, Silent Spring (1962) and with a growing retrospective acknowledgement of the contributions made by Thoreau, John Muir, John Ruskin and others, there has been a re-assessment of the relationship between human beings and their environment, between people and nature. I'd like to consider a particular aspect of this re-assessment: the sense in which we can feel at home in, and on, the earth, and the ways in which this at-homeness can generate changes in the way that we think about ourselves.

The terms 'kith' and 'kin' provide us with a useful opening into a discussion of home and relatedness. The word 'kith' comes from the Old English *cyththth*, meaning: 'knowledge, information; one's native land or region, home'.[1] In other words: the place we know, where we feel at home. The word 'kin' comes from the Old English *cyn(n)*, meaning: 'family or blood relations; a group of people descended from a common ancestry'.[2] Even from these bald dictionary definitions we can see that rather than being an expression of parochiality, exclusivity and chauvinism, 'kith and kin' can be an expression of relationship, inclusivity and community – an acknowledgement of common-landedness and common inheritance. For if we learn anything from ecological studies it is that the web of life is a web of interdependence and co-habitation - all beings sustained by interwoven natural systems within the atmospheric nest of the earth - complex ecological dynamics condensed in Gary Snyder's phrase, 'Earth House Hold'.[3]

*

Findings from recent studies in palaeo-anthropology and genetics confirm earlier speculations that the whole of humanity, now exceeding seven billion, evolved from one population of hominids living in East Africa. Based on evidence from more than a quarter of a million samples from around the world, geneticists have traced the migratory routes of these ancestors of ours, leaving Africa around 70,000 years ago and moving through southern Asia and into Australia about 50,000 years ago, into the colder climes of Europe about 40,000 years ago and eventually reaching the Americas. Genetic traces of more localised interactions between different populations are also being discovered. For instance, the genetic trace of 11th-century European crusaders is evident in modern Lebanese men; a similar legacy left by Genghis Khan and his followers can be found in the central Asian regions where they fought; and traces of Viking genes are found in very localised contemporary communities around the coasts of Britain.[4] We are all one extended family – widely dispersed, often fractious and, at times, divided by beliefs, values and aspirations – but one family nonetheless.

As I've argued in Chapter II, the boundaries between humans and other living beings, and between our individual bodies and the surrounding environment, are much less definite and fixed than we often think. Again recent studies, this time in genetics and bacteriology, suggest that we are each of us, in a very precise sense, a community of organisms rather than one organism. For instance, our skin is home to a diversity of microbes distributed in different densities around our bodies. The geneticist, Julia Segre, likens the human skin to the surface of the earth, broadly comprising three ecological habitats: moist, oily and dry – each with a distinctive community of bacteria, feeding off and interacting with their immediate surroundings.[5] Segre likens an armpit to a rainforest, a forearm to a desert and a navel to a rich oasis of life. As Steven Connor suggests, 'most skin bacteria do no harm and are likely to keep the skin healthy by preventing infections by more harmful microbes'.[6] Connor adds that 'bacterial cells are about 1,000 times smaller than human cells but far more numerous' – there are probably about ten times more bacterial cells in, and on, the human body than human cells. This may seem alarming but it is also reassuring. Each of us does not stand alone! We are many, not one – a community of interdependent organisms sharing the same body, just as, on a vaster scale, all beings share the same body of the earth.

It is important that we absorb these findings and add them to the teachings of many philosophical and religious traditions from around the world. For a sense of kith- and kin-ship carries with it a sense of mutuality and shared residency. If we are not only interrelated and porous communities of cells and microbes, through which genetic codes are transmitted, life is experienced and intentions are articulated, we are also needful of, and necessary to, each other. This ought to lead us, if not to the daily practice of tolerance and compassion, then at least to the aspiration for such tolerance and compassion.

*

To develop this connection between kinship and compassion let us return to Heidegger, that most elusive of thinkers. I've already discussed some of Heidegger's ideas about the self but I'd like to reflect again on what Heidegger has to say about the self as a site of being, what he refers to as, *Dasein* or 'being-here'. For Heidegger, *Dasein* is both a clearing or opening, a place in which possibilities arise and, more importantly the act of clearing or opening – clearing a space in which entities or phenomena can *be*. *Dasein* is always being-*in*-the-world, being as a participatory act, a relating to, and being part of, the warp and weft of the world. It's worth reading again what Barrett has to say:

> My Being is not something that takes place inside my skin (or inside an immaterial substance inside that skin); my Being, rather, is spread over a field or region which is the world of its care and concern.[7]

For Heidegger the space of Dasein is also a social space, 'being-here or there' is also 'being-with', we are bound together in Dasein, we are overlapping fields of 'care and concern'.

Barrett calls this a 'Field Theory of Being'. (ibid) In other words we are inhabitants of the world not spectators. We are implicated in what goes on around us, indeed 'what goes on around' is *part of* our being. Just as we are biologically a constellation of atoms, genes, cells, microbes, tissues and bones, we are existentially and philosophically an unfolding of ideas, images, stories and songs, a meeting place of countless threads of narrative, tradition and culture. If we can let go of our Cartesian, conditional, dualistic sense of self we can open up to this other way of being. Zimmerman writes:

> Freed from such dualism, people can enter into a new, nondomineering relationship with all things. Humans can encounter birds and trees, lakes and sky, humans and mountains not as independent, substantial, self-enclosed entities, but rather as temporary constellations of appearances: self-giving phenomena arising simultaneously.[8]

*

We can approach these ideas of how we relate to the world from other perspectives – from the viewpoint of the poet, hunter and shaman. At the end of the sixties I came across the poet Gary Snyder's description of still-hunting, a technique used by many indigenous peoples around the world:

> To hunt means to use your body and senses to the fullest: to strain your consciousness to feel what the deer are thinking today, this moment; to sit still and let yourself go into the birds and wind while waiting by a game trail.[9]

Snyder argues that poetry (and meditation practices such as *zazen* – see chapters X and XIV) are closely aligned to the ancient practices of hunting and shamanic ritual, each discipline sharing a common experience: a heightened perception of the phenomenal world, made possible by the dissolving of illusory boundaries between self and surroundings. He writes: 'everything was alive – the trees, grasses, and winds were dancing with me; I could understand the songs of the birds.'[10]

*

In many shamanic and oral cultures there tends to be a close association between song, poetry and a journeying to, and from, another realm – that is, a projective vision, an imaginative transformation, in which art (the making of song or poetry) is either the agency, and/or the recording, of journeying – a 'spiritual' or metaphysical travelogue. Geronimo, the Apache leader, tells Natalie Curtis, the ethnomusicologist:

> As I sing, I go through the air to a holy place where [the Supreme Being] will give me power to do wonderful things. I am surrounded by little clouds, and as I go through the air I change, becoming spirit only.'[11]

What a lucid and compelling way to describe the act of singing and poetry-making – as modes of projective flight and transformation. Halifax (ibid) notes that 'the shaman who desires a song does not fix his or her mind on particular words nor sing a known tune.' Rather, the shaman singer/poet/artist, acts as a vehicle, an opening or clearing (as Heidegger might put it), through which song, poem or image arises. No doubt many shamanic artists would go along with Hugh Kenner's view that T.S. Eliot, and other poets, aren't the originators of poems that somehow express their 'own' position[12] – rather they give voice to an 'other' – or the 'outside' as the poet Jack Spicer maintains.[13]

*

I now want to step sideways for a moment to consider another line of thought. If we shift our perspective from that of a conditional, unitary, Cartesian self to that of an open, more sustainable, porous self, we are embracing a much broader idea of kith and kin even than the one I outlined above. Not only do we move to a much wider sense of kith as including the whole 'earth house hold', we also move to an extended sense of kin to include not only the whole human family but also the communities of organisms, large and small, with which we maintain kinship based on indefinite boundaries, interdependence and shared habitats. This means we need to think about not only the intermingling of minds within the human domain but learn from the intermingling of cultures and modes of being of *all* beings.

George Steiner has some interesting things to say about the evolutionary role of languages and narrative codes within diverse human cultures. Firstly, he asks a straightforward question: why are there so many human languages? Even amongst peoples who share the same climatic and environmental conditions and who may only live a few miles apart, radically different linguistic forms have developed. Surely the frictions caused by mis-communication make this kind of diversity counter-productive? Steiner argues that the opposite is true: the emergence of many different languages has been crucial to human survival. Each language provides a different way of conceptualising the world. According to Steiner:

> [it is the] capacity of grammars to generate counter-factuals, 'if'-propositions and, above all, future tenses, which have empowered our species to hope, to reach far beyond the extinction of the individual.[14]

That is, humans can plan, imagine, speculate, and project into the future. We can visualise alternatives and possibilities and share our different visualisations through language – poetry, prose, art, music, drama and dance. Steiner goes on to suggest that:

> we endure creatively due to our imperative ability to say 'No' to reality, to build fictions of alterity, of dreamt or willed or awaited 'otherness' for our consciousness to inhabit.[15]

Through symbolic codes of infinite variety we can imagine alternative realities, propose alternative interpretations of these realities and present these interpretations to each other for reflection, debate, disagreement and further imaginative construction. For Steiner, each language represents, or enacts, a different mapping or interpretation of the world, and

> when a language dies, a possible world dies with it [....] Even when it is spoken by a handful, by the harried remnants of destroyed communities, a language contains within itself the boundless potential of discovery, of recompositions of reality, of articulate dreams, which are known to us as myths, as poetry, as metaphysical conjecture and the discourse[s] of law.[16]

In keeping with our revised notions of kith and kin, we can extend and apply Steiner's thinking to include the symbol structures and communication systems of mammals, insects and birds, and the information-processing and sharing systems of other organisms. The world is a hubbub of languages, of songs and stories, dances and images, woven into the air and waters, inscribed on the land, reaching into the past and the future. Maybe we should revise Teilhard de Chardin's concept of the *noosphere* to include not only the realm of collective human thought but also the infinitely varied cognitive and information-processing structures of all beings.[17]

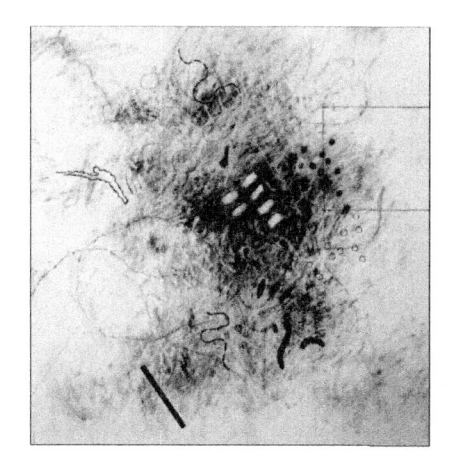

The robin weaving a watery song in the morning air, the snail inscribing his fluid trail on the dry pavement, James Lovelock articulating some aspect of Gaia theory, Bjork singing a complex melody or a skateboarder performing a new trick – these are all examples of invention and adaptability. As are the mutations of a virus in response to changing conditions or the slow ponderous music of mountains rising or falling over millions of year. All of these counter-factual discourses, interpretations, ways of doing and being, constitute the cultural heritage of the earth – the narratives and dreams of our kith and kin. This is the great storehouse of knowledge and practices that we inherit, revise, extend and pass on to future generations. It is in this dynamic, shape-shifting storehouse, that we work and play – this is our home.

If our view of ourselves is rooted in a deep sense of mutuality with all forms of existence – a deep sense of kith and kinship with our fellow inhabitants of the earth – it becomes vital that we sustain this wonderful polyphony of cultures and languages, human and non-human – the dappled music of fibre, flesh and bone.

*

The German protestant shoemaker and theologian, Jacob Boehme (1575-1625), in his book, *Signatura Rerum* – 'the signature of all things' – put forward the idea that everything in nature is a manifestation of God's infinite being. A similar idea is implicit in the writings of the poets Henry Vaughan and Ronald Johnson. R.A. Durr suggests that for Henry Vaughan (1621/2-1695)) nature was *liber creatorum*, 'a system of divine hieroglyphs'.[18] Durr describes Vaughan's poems as 'sparks from the flint'[19] and we can see both sparks and flint in the poem, The Morning-watch:

> [....] the quick world
> Awakes, and sings;
> The rising winds,
> And falling springs,
> Birds, beasts, all things
> Adore him in their kinds.

> Thus all is hurl'd
> In sacred *Hymnes*, and *Order*, The great *Chime*
> And *Symphony* of nature.[20]

Here Vaughan seems to be reading the book of creation and interpreting its 'divine hieroglyphs' in crystalline imagery. Though Vaughan enjoyed those moments of 'living where the Sun / Doth all things wake', he also recognised that, 'There is in God (some say) / A deep, but dazzling darkness', and the darkness of God is a place of solace and peace.[21] Indeed, Vaughan yearns for 'that night! where I in him / Might live invisible and dim'.[22]

Something of the same spirit of finding a Godly or sacred dimension to nature can be found in the early poetry of Ronald Johnson. Johnson was born in a small town in Kansas in 1935 and in 1962-63 he spent a year travelling around England, often walking, visiting places that had particular associations with poetry and literature. His first book of poems, The Book of the Green Man,[23] is a record of the physical and imaginative journey undertaken by the young poet, who seems to have one foot in the seventeenth century world of Henry Vaughan and George Herbert, and the other foot in his own century. The poems in The Book of the Green Man are dappled with references to the Metaphysical Poets, William Wordsworth, John Clare, Greek myths and to the painter, Samuel Palmer.

Johnson's poem, What the Leaf Told Me, begins with a quotation from the diaries of the nineteenth century writer, Francis Kilvert: 'Today I saw the word written on the poplar leaves. / It was 'dazzle'. The dazzle of the poplars'.[24] This is a springboard for one of many meditations on the idea of nature as scripture, the natural world as a sacred writing. The poem continues:

> As a leaf startles out
>
> from an undifferentiated mass of foliage,
> so the word did from a leaf –
>
> A mirage Of The Delicate Polyglot

inventing itself as cipher. But this, in shifts & gyrations, grew in brightness, so bright

the massy poplars soon outshone the sun ...

'My light – my dews – my breezes – my bloom'. Reflections

In A Wren's Eye.[25]

The diversity of nature generates a diversity of languages and tongues, each of which encodes a particular thought or narrative - a fragment of the cosmic narrative that constitutes God's natural scripture. Johnson sets out to decipher some of these coded manifestations of God's discourse, sometimes through a deep empathic identification with natural forms and events - for example the line 'I am a walking fire, I am all leaves', which he takes from Edith Sitwell's poem, The Song of the Cold.[26] On other occasions the deciphering is a process of meditation, even yearning:

I wish
for this earth, beneath
to move, to issue some dark, meditated

syllable perhaps –

something more
than this inarticulate

warble
& seething.[27]

This extract comes from the opening passage of the Winter section of the book. Johnson walks in the Lake District, thinking about Wordsworth who, he hopes, still inhabits the ground on which he walks. But the above lines continue with Johnson's sad acknowledgement that, 'this soil, once / Wordsworth, lies / in silence'.[28] On this occasion at least there is no 'dark [...] syllable' to interpret. Wordsworth is mute and the young Johnson has to wander on, looking elsewhere for signs of sacred poetry.

---

[1] Anon 2002: 1503
[2] *ibid*: 1497
[3] Snyder 1969
[4] see McKie 2008: 16
[5] see Connor 2009: 13
[6] *ibid*
[7] Barrett 1990: 217
[8] in Guignon 1993: 262
[9] Snyder 1969: 120
[10] *ibid*: 123
[11] in Halifax 1991: 32
[12] Kenner 1965: 37
[13] see Blaser 1975
[14] Steiner 1998: xiv
[15] *ibid*
[16] *ibid*
[17] see Teilhard de Chardin 2008
[18] Durr 1962: 19
[19] *ibid*: 11
[20] in Gardner 1966: 267
[21] *ibid*: 281
[22] *ibid*
[23] Johnson 1967
[24] *ibid*: 54
[25] *ibid*
[26] *ibid*: 38
[27] *ibid*: 17
[28] *ibid*

60 Interwoven Nature

V. THE OLD MAN LOOKS AROUND

The worm turns and I can feel his turning. The buzzard pirouettes slowly above me and I can feel his roving gaze pass over my upturned face. And I can feel his disinterest, the dull neutrality of his eyes as he searches for prey. I listen to the deer, the wood mouse, the grass snake and the butterfly. Even though they rarely make a sound I come to realise they have a lot to say.

Around me the beech buds are fattening. Over the valley white smoke drifts across squalls of bramble and blackthorn. Dog droppings mark the meadow walk. A pigeon feather lies at the entrance to the badger diggings. I look up at the webbed limbs of golden ash. The sun sets slowly and I remember other sunsets at other places: logs floating on the Pacific shoreline, deadfall from the groves of pine and cypress; a wooden jetty on the Brisbane river, pelicans coming in to land like 1930s flying boats, the glistening city like a promised land; rocks like an old man and woman standing with hunched shoulders in needle rain, silhouetted against a pale sky; a coyote, limping, moving wearily through ponderosa pines in a Colorado park; frogs croaking like geese, hidden in ditches in a glade of willows and alder in the Marais Poitevin region of southern Brittany. They come to mind like migrating swans, passing through on their way to other climes.

It's evening. I sit in the wood and watch a pair of bats skittering in and out of the turkey oaks, swooping and flapping over the house, tilting their weightless bodies in the synchronised jagged flight patterns of the hardly visible insects they chase. Every now and then they dissolve into the darkness of the Monterey pines. The drowsy air is startled by their jerky elegance and I marvel that such skill and confidence can flow from these tiny bundles of skin-shrouded intelligence.

I've tried to heed the advice of my old friend, Charles Waterton, now long gone, who said, 'look close with a quiet mind.' Quietening the mind used to be difficult as it seemed always full of mosquitoes and chirruping larks, but now it comes easy and the creatures around me don't seem to notice my watchfulness. Sometimes days go by and I forget who I am, yet this forgetting leaves me more alive to the world, able to feel the shivering of the frosted leaves and the churning motion of the mole beneath my feet. Sitting still, without the burden of name and history, is one of life's great gifts, a treasure-trove of sights, sounds and meetings.

Another old friend, Jacob Boehme, who was the mildest of men and very knowledgeable about shoes and their manufacture, wrote me a letter advising me to give up searching and striving and running after exotic sights and look more closely at my own patch of earth. His words come to me now: 'the true heaven is everywhere, even in that very place where thou standest and goest.' Jacob had a special penchant for sunbeams, he would sit and stare at motes of dust dancing in the light, saying, 'these are the only angels that matter. See how in the lowliest of things there is great beauty that enlivens and calms the mind. Sit quiet where you are and watch the dusty angels.'

Sometimes I sit for so long spiders spin their webs over my ears and occasionally over my eyes. I can see the silver threads gathering, twisting light into an intricate geometry. I can feel the tension in the threads as they quiver at each footfall of the arachnid at work. Sometimes I can hear the frail music of flies in the dusty air, working out how to avoid the spider traps, puzzling their way to a window or a door, careful to avoid the deadly touch of wonder. Some days I get entranced by the detritus that builds up on every surface that doesn't receive the sweep of a brush or the stroke of a cloth. Indeterminate fields of dust and delight. Windowsills are always a rich graveyard of dishevelled insects - flies, moths, unlucky bees, furious wasps. I gather up these discarded husks and tip them out on to a sheet of paper to examine them. I admire their intricacy and delicate enduring beauty. The happenstance jumble of bodies always looks like a long forgotten script, a message waiting to be deciphered, a story waiting to be told.

On a sunny afternoon I lie next to the pond watching a grass snake glide through the purple loosestrife and cotton grass, over the pebbles and into the water. There's hardly a ripple. This is a regular jaunt in hot weather. In the clear water I can count about twenty common newts floating at different levels with their legs and toes splayed out, perfectly still yet seemingly alert to the predator in their midst. After a while I notice the snake's head peering out, the pale yellow band around his neck perfectly aligned with the surface of the water, wonderfully camouflaged, tongue flicking as if in disdain at my earlier attempts to find him with a gently *prodding stick. I'm always surprised that the newts don't abandon the small pond, scattering into the surrounding vegetation. But they don't. Some understanding binds them to the water and to the snake's ancient charm. I wonder how many newts a grass snake can eat in one sitting?*

Even at midday a tawny owl hoots. Deer tracks harden in drying mud. Bees dance a complex jig as the willow blossoms nod in the breeze. Overhead a buzzard mews, cutting the fabric of the hour.

There is so much life shimmering in every nook and cranny of the earth, in the fervent waters and in the uplifting air, it is hard to know how so many variations of form and voice and temper have emerged out of the chemical storehouse that is our planet. I remember some words of Gerard Manley Hopkins, who seems as puzzled as anyone by what he sees around him: 'where does all this throng and stack of being, so rich, so distinctive, come from / nothing I see can answer me'.[1]

As I sit here I watch and lose myself in the watching, emptying into the world like a trickle of rainwater disappearing into the roadside grasses. As the day opens its eyes what is there to see?

>   rooks gathering
>   in dark pines
>   as dawnlight
>   pinks the air
>
>   a few leaves
>   on the Judas Tree
>   still hang like
>   yellow sails
>
>   city in mist
>   lies low
>   a band
>   of silver grey
>   hides all those people
>   all that noise

Wherever I look life has scribbled its playful notes upon every surface - scriptures written in chlorophyll and flesh. A force that started long ago, in the chemistry of the earth's early years, spins out its momentum in an infinite variety of experiments and doodles, shaping matter into forms that can repeat themselves with endless melodic variations - cosmic improvisations of atoms, genes, cells, and every note on the scale of substance, never stopping to draw breath or admire its own handiwork. There is no rhyme or reason to this process beyond the rhyme and reason of its own generative impulse. This is not a performance done to prove a point or to exemplify a theorem or justify a belief. There is no mind outside this serendipitous process that watches with pride or regret to see what happens, no composer or master-of-ceremonies who directs the flow of events and forms. There is no one to blame or praise for the way life unfolds. All we can do is bear witness to its fecund majesty, to be grateful for every vagrant smudge of living matter that greets our senses, be awake to what is all around us and do what we can to take care of it.

...every vagrant smudge of life....

[1] Hopkins 1963: 145

66 Interwoven Nature

VI. INTERMINGLING MINDS

> 'There is one mind common to all individual men.
> Every man is an inlet of the same and to all of the same.'
> (Emerson, essay on History, 1911: 5)

In this chapter I'd like to take a different approach to ideas about identity, subjectivity and mind touched on in earlier chapters. I'm going to take the image and locus of Venice as a crossroads and use it as a metaphor with which to discuss culture and language as an intermingling of minds.

Just as snails leave trails, sheep leave tracks across hillsides (sometimes centuries old), and badgers and foxes wear smooth the routes they take through grass and hedgerows, so we humans leave traces of our peregrinations. The surface of the earth is criss-crossed by routes taken by adventurous women and men on journeys of trading and discovery. These journeys exemplify ways in which human beings interact with, and weave through, each other and the environment. Evidence of the routes of these journeys can be found in the form of paths, roads and settlements, and in the signs, charts and stories that mark these pathways. The physical trails that weave in and out of each other across the planet are layered in time and are closely aligned with the memories and narratives that record and celebrate such journeys.

Many towns and cities have grown at the places where important routes begin, end and cross over each other. These places become centres of trade, discovery, communication and artistic exchange. They develop distinctive cultural identities and influence, and interact with, other places in a region and further afield. Venice is one example of such a centre, and can be seen as an important crossroads *and process* whereby minds interact, interweave and transform each other. Venice, and other trading crossroads, can also be seen as a metaphor for the human mind, which is itself a crossroads of currents of causality, thought, feeling and sensation – a cultural axis through which, and from which, ideas and images flow.

Every human being, like Venice, moves at the shifting centre of infinite vectors of thoughts, feelings, narratives, possibilities and histories – currents and migrations of identity that cross paths in this embodied mind we call *me, myself,* (or *Venice*). Just as Venice is a confluence of travels, pilgrimages and tradings between peoples, ages and ideas, so are we. The mind of Venice, like the mind of any of us, and the mind which is all of us, is a cosmopolis that we somehow tend to think of as a monopolis. We forget the manifold intricacy of the crossings, the comings and goings of people, in order to preserve a portmanteau myth - which is that Venice, like each of us, is one entity, place or name – a unitary some*thing* rather than a polymorphous process. How mistaken we are in wishing to replace the ceaseless motion of multitudes with the steady fixity of one, or misreading the layered tracks of the many for a single grave with one name on its solitary tombstone.

*

There is a well-known photograph by an unknown photographer of the imposing marble staircase of the Ca'Rezzonico in Venice. This is the *palazzo* in which Robert Browning died in 1889. It is thought that the sombre bowler-hatted figure climbing the staircase is Browning himself, darkly ascending to the light-filled window. This is one of the few 'sunprints' we have of Browning. It was taken in the year of his death.

Stairways of all kinds lead us upwards and downwards, in and out of the light, between one space and another. They are *skyladders*, in the shamanic sense, enabling us to move from one to another of the stratified realms of existence, and also they are indexical signs of our passage through these realms. They are both stairways to heaven and footfalls to hell.

Near the end of his own life Guy Davenport recounts a confluence of lives and deaths around a staircase in Rome. Davenport tells us that Joan Severn was the cousin of John Ruskin. During the last decade of his life Ruskin was immured in the madness that had afflicted him for brief periods in his earlier days. Only occasionally would he find himself in the light, able to recognise his cousin. The rest of the time she was a stranger, passing him from time to time on the stairs. Davenport writes:

> In 1871 Joan Agnew, as she then was, had married the son of Joseph Severn who closed Keats's [dead] eyes. Ruskin had met Joseph Severn on a staircase in Rome in 1841, Ruskin ascending, Severn and George Richmond descending. Richmond had closed the eyes of William Blake.[1]

In this ascending and descending we recognise an obvious, yet powerful, metaphor for the passage of a life. And in the gentle closing of one persons' eyes by another we recognise the closing of a light-filled window on to the world and into an unfathomable mind. In much the same way the shutter of a heavy camera opened and closed on Browning's dark form as it rose like a bird in slow-motion through the stairwell of a Venetian palazzo.

*

Ralph Waldo Emerson, who, apart from his many lecture tours in the USA and abroad, lived most of his life in Concord, Massachusetts, is not much read today. This almost universal neglect is perhaps indicative of his universal relevance. He has much to say to us. Couched in the pantheistic language of transcendentalism he speaks of the divinity of every being and the sacred connectedness of every thought, whoever thinks it. To Emerson there is one universal mind within which all that has been, is, and can be thought, occurs. In this sense we are interwoven beings, inter-minded and inter-feeling. We share a common history of thought, feeling, perception and aspiration. For Emerson this belief in a universal mind, or at least a common ancestry of intermingled ideas and feelings, can be taken as an indication of a shared right of access to a common humanity: 'What Plato has thought, [every man] may think; what a saint has felt, he may feel; what at any time has befallen any man, he can understand.'[2]

In the second half of the nineteenth century Emerson was famous and influential across America and Europe. The Argentine poet Jorge Luis Borges writes that Nietzsche, who often visited Venice, 'felt himself so close to Emerson that he did not dare to praise him because it would have been like praising himself'.[3] Despite, or because of, his universalism and his teaching that all is one, Emerson was also drawn to scepticism and an almost Heraclitean delight in paradox and contradiction. Borges quotes from Emerson's poem, *Brahma*,

> Far or forgot to me is near;
>   Shadow and sunlight are the same;
> The vanished gods to me appear;
>   And one to me are shame and fame.[4]

This 'coincidence of opposites', to use Nicolas of Cusa's phrase, is echoed in the way in which disparate groups of human beings are bound together through the inter-related languages they speak.

Both Emerson and Borges would probably have agreed with the idea that we are all multi-perspectival creatures, co-ordinates of many trajectories (social, psychological, historical, biological, cultural), convergences and divergences of thoughts, sensations, narratives and moods. We are pages in an open book that has no binding and we are the writings that appear on those pages.

The threads of our thinking are often invisible, as slender as gossamer, and the threads are coextensive with our sensations and the makings of our hands, and with what we read and what the world entwines us in and in us.

*

I overhear two Dutchmen talking in a hotel in Aberdeen. They discuss how, in Surinam, many families live together in large communal buildings. When some of these families emigrated to Holland in the 1960s, they were housed in large blocks of flats. Quite soon after they arrived, neighbours reported hearing lots of hammering and drilling and rubble was seen being taken away. It came to light that they had been knocking down the walls between apartments and drilling holes in floors and ceilings in order to be able to talk to each other and to see and interact with their neighbours. They brought with them ideas and practices of community, housing and living that were very different to the northern Netherlanders. Houses had to become more porous and spaces more fluid in order for their new homes to be habitable. For the Surinamese, a house is a site at the confluence of many family lines and histories, a crossing point, a conversational domain in which many bloodlines converge.

*

Robert Duncan, in The Venice Poem, writes: 'I am like an empty shell / tortured with voices. / Alone, I know not where I am. / I cry out. / My voices answer.'[5] For Duncan the making of poetry is a dialogue between voices. He sometimes refers to these voices as 'companions', and it is the conversations with these companions that establish Duncan's polyvocal identity as a poet. There is nothing new in this. Indeed Duncan is continuing a tradition that extends back through time and outwards geographically. Celtic bards, Judeo-Christian prophets, Sufi mystics, Romantic poets and tribal seers have all espoused the same notion – that they are moved by a confluence of forces, currents of story, song and image that pass through them, temporarily illuminating the openings, the clearings (as Heidegger might say) – the potential to be, which is what we are – each of us a resonating energy field of consciousness, awakening and imagination.

Duncan's circle of poet friends includes Jack Spicer and Robin Blaser, who both speak of poetry as a giving voice to the Other (Duncan's 'companions'). Blaser writes: 'A *reopened language* [poetry] lets the unknown, the Other, the outside in again as a voice in the language'.[6] Later, he adds:

It is within language that the world speaks to us with a voice that is not our own. This is, I believe, a first and fundamental experience of dictation and correspondence – the speaking to us in language is only one level of the outside that ceaselessly invades our thought.[7]

The poet's role is to take down the dictation of the world in all its multiple voices, registers and modes. As Blaser argues, 'the poem's real business, [is] an 'exhibition of world' (Heidegger)'.[8]

Yet, paradoxically, the Other is, or the Others are, what we are. It is the others within that are also the Outside. The Outside is also the Inside. The self is no longer an impermeable essence, separate from everything else. Instead, it is a permeable, fluid process, a confluence of voices, images and histories. The self is polyvocal and polymorphous.

*

We can trace many of these currents of thought and sensibility in the work of the American poet, Ezra Pound (who died in the autumn of 1972 in Venice), particularly as elucidated by Hugh Kenner in his seminal book, The Pound Era. Writing about The Waste Land, Ulysses and the Cantos – early iconic literary modernism – Kenner suggests that the 'province of these works [...] is the entire human race speaking, and in time as well as space'.[9] He notes the borrowings from 'Greek, Latin, Chinese, Italian, French, Provencal, Spanish, Arabic and Egyptian Hieroglyphic languages'.[10] Pound's mind acts as a conduit and a meeting place - a watering hole for long dead scholar monks and parched troubadours. Pound's synaptic energy-field of association, cross-reference and cryptic conviviality acts like the perfect innkeeper in the perfect inn - bringing together travellers, émigrés, roustabouts and songbirds from all ages and regions. Pound argued that, 'All ages are contemporaneous in the mind'.[11]

Venice seems an appropriate place for Pound to end his days – a suitable crossroads at which this innkeeper could gather images, phrases, flourishes of opinion and ideas that could be woven into poetry by his restless and much-travelled mind. And if we listen at the door of Pound's poetry inn, we hear the polyglot music of cultural migrations and exchanges, borrowings and trade. No wonder translation and transposition occupied so much of Pound's time.

Kenner writes of Pound's ability to register both diversity and etymological evolution: 'This aplomb amid the multitudinous tongues of the world [...] amid testimony to their constant change'.[12] In Pound's work we find both a layered cultural geology and an analogical rendering of the complexity of consciousness. Currents of ideas in many voices, channelled through an individual (be it Joyce, Eliot or Pound) give us the tone, dynamics and divergences that make up the provenance of Sappho's 'spangled mind' – to use Anne Carson's resonant term.[13] This is not mind as a container or cave, but mind as a stream into which countless rivulets run and in which the surrounding territory is dipped, mirrored and dappled and thrown back at itself in infinitely varied reflections and refractions. It is this multifarious resonance that gives Pound's poem-as-mind, or mind-as-poem, its sense of being in, or passing through, a particular time and place. There is a history inscribed in each poem, phrase, quotation and translation - a genealogy of hybridisation, cross-pollination and mutuality that gives us a genetic profile of human syntax and semantics.

In Pound's thinking and writing, in the conundrum known as *Ezra Pound*, and in each poem that articulates Pound's flux of identity or self-making, we find a linguistic archaeology of being, imagining and mind. As Kenner observes, in Pound's poetry, 'the filaments run back in time [...] binding us all to our dead ancestors'.[14] There is a sense in which Pound may have agreed with Emerson in believing that the mind is not coextensive with any particular body, but is embodied, in some way shared, by many bodies – perhaps by all bodies. Maybe this is what Joyce means by his reference to philology as the 'strandentwining cable of all flesh'.[15] Kenner goes on:

> We are joined [...] as much to one another as to the dead by continuities of speech as of flesh.[16]

*

To digress slightly, it seems likely that many of the languages which Europeans have employed to argue, disagree and fight about ideas of God, territory and power, share Indo-European roots. It is a satisfying irony that the fear or dislike of the supposedly *alien* cultures of Asia, particularly the Indian sub-continent, which has haunted Europeans for centuries, is expressed in languages which have evolved from the same roots as Sanskrit, the language of the Vedic hymns of India. As Melvyn Bragg points out:

> The similarities are remarkable. In Sanskrit the word for father is 'pitar'; in Greek and Latin it is 'pater'; in German, 'Vater'; in English, 'father'. 'Brother' is English, the Dutch is 'broeder', in German 'Bruder', in Sanskrit 'bhratar'. There can be few clearer examples of the spread and flow of language and the interconnection of peoples.[17]

Likewise the Latin, 'vox', the English, 'voice', and the Sanskrit, 'vak', issue from the same philological source.[18]

While languages often put down local roots, taking on characteristics of grammar, tone and register that have a geographical locus, they are also inextricably interwoven with each other, sharing ancestry with currents of expression that may stretch over many thousands of miles. Venice, where Pound lived the last years of his life, can be seen as emblematic of this paradoxical notion that while we occupy space, while we are some*where*, grounded here or there, we are also porous and, at times, transparent, open eyed and minded to the influx of the world and its inhabitants trailing their tangled histories like so many comets across the dark sky.

In a poem entitled, Everness, in Richard Wilbur's translation, Jorge Luis Borges writes:

> One thing does not exist: Oblivion.
> God saves the metal and he saves the dross,
> And his prophetic memory guards from loss
> The moons to come, and those of evenings gone.
> Everything *is*: the shadows in the glass

> Which, in between the day's two twilights, you
> Have scattered by the thousands, or shall strew
> Henceforward in the mirrors that you pass.
> And everything is part of that diverse
> Crystalline memory, the universe; ...[19]

Borges, like Pound and Emerson, gives us the idea that the present contains all histories, the individual mirrors in some way *all* individuals, each mind reflects every other mind. Each of us is a confluence of interpenetrating thoughts, feelings, atoms and genetic codes – labyrinthine in complexity and hybridity.

*

The Inuit, as the indigenous Eskimos of the far north call themselves, trace their ancestry back through language to a common source, as do many other peoples around the world. Their collective memory brings to mind a mode of being that is both human *and* animal. Joyce's 'strandentwining cable of all flesh', is of *all* flesh, and reaches far, far back in time. The great Danish collector of shamanic tales and songs, Knud Rasmussen, travelled through the arctic homelands of the Inuit from Siberia to Greenland in the early years of the twentieth century. He collected the following statement of origins from Nalungiaq, a Netsilik woman. It was then reworked as a poem in English by Edward Field in the nineteen-sixties:

> *Magic Words* (after Nalungiaq)
>
> In the very earliest time,
> when both people and animals lived on the earth,
> a person could become an animal if he wanted to
> and an animal could become a human being.
> Sometimes they were people
> and sometimes animals
> and there was no difference.
> All spoke the same language.
> That was the time when words were like magic.
> The human mind had mysterious powers.[20]

strandentwining memory

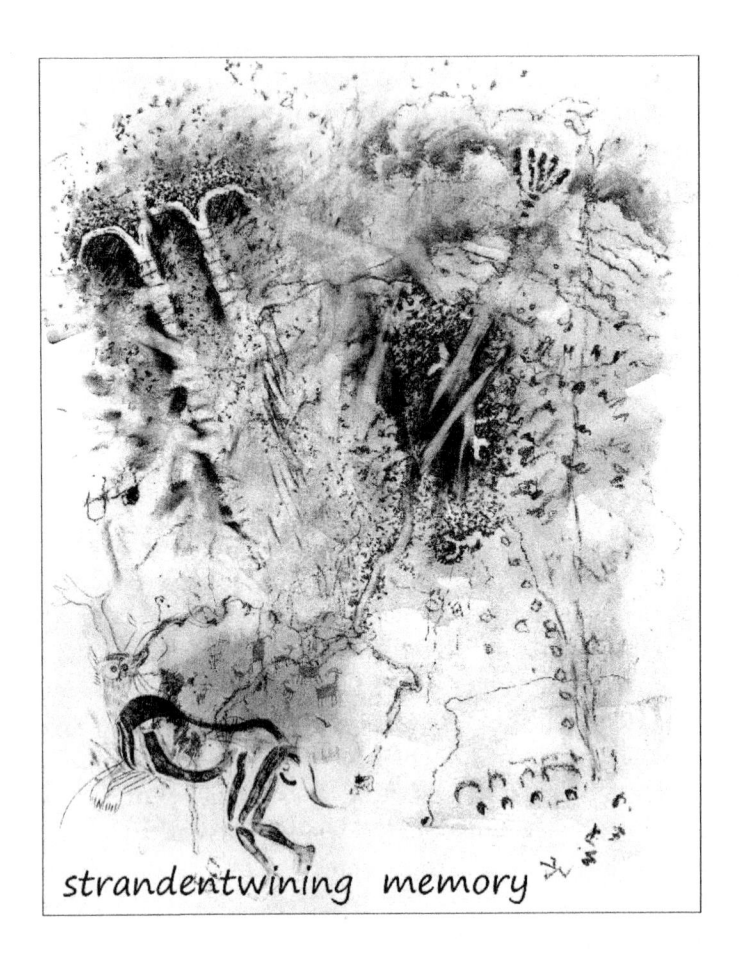

Perhaps this channel of oral literature leads back further through wordless 'sound poems' (of which there are countless examples from tribal cultures around the world) to silent pictographs, and to the symbolic, iconic and indexical signs, dating back thirty to forty thousand years, found at Palaeolithic sites across the globe.

Many sound-poems are explained by those who compose or recite them as the words of animals or spirits, or even as the remains of an ancestral language whose meaning has been lost. Here is an Australian Aborigine sound-poem, transcribed from an oral performance by Baldwin Spencer:

Dad a dad a
Dad a dad a
Dad a dad a
Da kata kai

Ded o ded o
Ded o ded o
Ded o ded o
Da kata kai[21]

*

Marco Polo is one of the most famous sons of Venice and probably its greatest traveller. He journeyed across Asia for nearly a quarter of a century and became an advisor to, and ambassador of, the Mongol leader of China, the great Kubla Khan - about whom Coleridge was to dream in an opium-induced sleep in 1897. Five hundred years earlier Polo wrote an account of his travels which became one of the most popular of medieval texts. Despite its credentials as a bestseller the book was often referred to as *Il Milione*, 'The Million Lies', and its author was given the nickname of Marco Milione. Many Europeans, perhaps most, considered his book as a fable rather than as an account of true events and places actually visited. Some even raised the possibility that Polo never went to China, citing as evidence the lack of reference in his writings to everyday phenomena like the binding of women's feet, calligraphy & tea, and the lack of any reference to Marco Polo in contemporary Chinese accounts of visitors and happenings at the Mongol court.[22]

These doubters prompt the thought that perhaps Polo only went to China in his mind. Maybe his travels were imaginative rather than physical, his writings fictional, or semi-fictional, rather than fact? Maybe Polo sat on board a vessel on the open sea reading other accounts of Chinamen and embellishing these with mental forays into unknown territory – from which he wove his own accounts of a China that was yet to be visited or constructed in the European imagination? Or maybe he never left Venice? Perhaps he sat in his study, high above the waterline, studying the shifting patterns of wave and light as they were set dancing by the passage of ships across the busy lagoon? Maybe this was enough to set his mind dancing to strange tunes played by strange instruments from a world upon which he had not set foot?

Or, perhaps, it is more credible to think of a Chinese traveller, one of the first to visit Europe, who lands unannounced in Venice, sent by Kubla Khan to report back on this strange land of pale-skinned foreigners. He meets up with Marco Polo in a drinking house and as they both slowly get drunk tells him, in the smattering of Italian, Latin and Turkish picked up en route, of his travels and of his homeland. Naturally, he describes all the unusual and exotic features of his country, never thinking that anyone would be interested in mundane details like the drinking of tea, the use of brush-drawn calligraphy or the binding of women's feet. As he describes his hometown of Hangzhou, he feels pangs of homesickness mixed with a curious sense of being at home. For Hangzhou is a city of lakes and canals and islands much like the city in which he now sits. He has travelled halfway around the world only to find himself in a marvellous translation of the city he left many years before. Perhaps, as he falls asleep, he smiles at this meeting of minds and reiteration of place, and looks across at the smiling face of his new Venetian friend who, in turn, is wondering whether anyone will believe the book he is about to write.

---

[1] Davenport 2003: 37
[2] Emerson 1911: 5
[3] Borges 1973: 25
[4] *ibid*: 26-2
[5] Duncan 1968: 83
[6] Blaser 1975: 276
[7] *ibid*: 279
[8] *ibid*: 282
[9] Kenner 1975: 95
[10] *ibid*
[11] in Rothenberg & Joris 1995: 733
[12] Kenner 1975: 95
[13] Carson 2003: 3 & 357
[14] Kenner 1975: 96
[15] *ibid*
[16] *ibid*: 96-97
[17] Bragg 2003: 4
[18] see Snyder 1975: 9
[19] Borges 1985: 207
[20] in Rothenberg 1972: 45
[21] in Rothenberg & Joris 1995: 742
[22] see Silk-road website 2011

up the ridge

wet rock

shale slides

VII. THE OLD MAN REMEMBERS AND PONDERS

I can remember when the butterflies on the heath were like confetti. As we ran through the bilberries and heather they fluttered in rapture like nuns at the visitation of a saint – a giddying declamation of winged prayers. They skipped from bush to bush and flower to flower like stars cut loose from the celestial order. We had to flick them out of our faces as we ran and when we sat down to rest on the tussocks of dry grass they would sit on us, flexing their wings, rolling out their proboscises to taste the afternoon air before catching flight again, dawdling uncertainly on unseen currents of navigation and indecision.

Day after day I'd be out walking - over the heathland, up the bracken slopes. Picking bilberries from the ankle-high bushes huddled between granite boulders. Catching great-crested newts in ponds by the old quarry. Climbing the sheer rock faces, where quarrymen like my father had drilled and blasted a huge wound into the hill. Small poems would come to mind as I walked - patterns of words tumbling out of the rhythmic motion of footfall and rest. Sometimes a title would settle on the nape of the poem, like this one: Gorse-gandering

>   *wet rock*
>   *& the fern tangle*
>   *knees gouged*
>
>   *spears of seeded grass*
>   *hang handles down*
>   *from my sweater*
>   *& jeans*
>
>   *up the gorse ridge*
>   *clay sticks to shoes as I*

peep between spikes
at cows & the far
outcrop

shale slides
flat decks of granite
quartz blocks jut out
& glint

high sun
peers into bottom quarry
shade

rock doves
hurl themselves
or fall
feet drawn up
beaks & necks
extended

Once out in the hills I met a woman in a pale blue coat who had lost her way. She was sitting on a rock gazing at the heather that was just coming into bloom. As we talked she held a sprig of blossom in her hand and turned it slowly from side to side, as if she was looking for something that could only be seen in a certain light. She told me that wherever she looked there were flowers: flowers of celebration, pain and remembrance; flowers of sky and of water; flowers of light and shade; flowers of hope and despair. When she walked in the darkness she could see flowers of moonlight with star-like petals. When she looked at roses she could hear the flowers of pleasure humming inside her. She said that behind every flower she could see there was another yet to be seen, and that there were always new flowers waiting in her dreams. Everywhere there were unnamed flowers yet to be named, named flowers yet to be unnamed. And this was her aim in life: to take away the names of flowers, for only then, she said quietly, can we see each flower for what it is. Though this seemed a foolish thing for a grown woman to be doing I couldn't help but take her seriously. There was something about her gentle resolve that stirred me to look at the heather more closely and to see it in a new light. I pointed down into the valley and told her that there was the track she needed to reach the road. As I got to the top of a rise I looked back to where she had been sitting. She wasn't there. I gazed down at the track winding down to the road but I still couldn't see her. As I walked on I noticed a figure far in front of me. It was a woman in a pale blue coat.

Some days the gorse would glow with a yellow that seemed unearthly, as if the visible spectrum had suddenly expanded to fit in a new fiery tone. Walking towards it, the dark mass of barbs would grow darker and more inhospitable, as if protecting the linnets that nested in its unfathomable reaches. The yellow seemed to me like a flag on a castle turret, as if the people besieged within, wanted to draw attention to their plight while at the same time telling the world that this was their place and they weren't going to leave without a fight. For though they could not fight, except by hiding, the linnets were besieged – by boys who collected their eggs, by magpies who occasionally found a way to steal the helpless chicks as they cowered in silence and by the gradual encroachment of the granite quarry that ate away at the patches of gorse. But we didn't know that back then. I was one of the boys, trying to add another small trophy to the collection of eggs my father had started in his youth. It all seems so petty and pointless now, a desecration of the heath that I loved, but then it was a passion – to watch and study the habits of birds so that they would lead us to their nests, to take just one egg and to tell our friends not to take another from that nest, and to sit at night gazing at the eggs arranged in the old wooden cigar box. Speckled, patterned and plain they seemed like jewels. We could see no reason to forego this pleasure or to recognise what folly it was to think there would always be more birds to find and more eggs to collect. Now, even though the quarry has been abandoned and the boys are long gone, linnets are rarely seen on the heath.

In those days I would help my father in the garden. It was a stony, black-soiled patch on a steep slope beneath the granite tor that fell away into the deep belly of the quarry. Dead-Man's Drop we called it. A narrow track skirted the quarry-side of the rocky summit. We would dare each other to walk along these five yards of thin frightening pathway – on one side the sheer flat wall of stone rising at our fingertips, on the other the few hundred feet of air at our feet. Our house was called Charnwood Knoll, after the granite tor at its head, and the garden stretched out to the south of the tor, edged with large boulders and bounded on three sides by the grasping bracken and the groves of young birch, pine and mountain ash. My father laboured in the evenings and at weekends, struggling to keep some sort of human order against the encroachment of weeds, seedling trees, wood pigeons and foxes. As he worked jackdaws would mutter and cry, chirring and squabbling, endlessly commenting on his labours. But his hard work was rewarded by good crops of potatoes, carrots, cabbages, runner beans, currants and raspberries, supplemented by delicious sweetly-scented tomatoes from the greenhouse and apples from the old trees that cast a speckled shade on the summer lawn. Listening to him talk about the craft of gardening was a great pleasure and I looked forward to the visits of my uncle Walter, knowing that when he called my father would have someone to talk to for hours about the virtues and vices of different varieties of vegetables and fruit, the merits and shortcomings of different ways of rearing dahlias and chrysanths, and the vicissitudes of weather, terrain, soil and season. I loved to hear them chattering, arguing and laughing – so like the jackdaws gathered around our chimneys. Sometimes a poem would emerge, like this one with a title that so pleased me: Pea-stick Rondo

> *chopping birch branches*
>
> *for pea-sticks you have*
> *to get them about three*
> *feet long   the smaller*
> *twigs forming something*
> *like a fan*
>
> *you point the thick end*
>
> *& clean the lower six*
> *inches of side-twigs*
> *so that you can push*
> *it into the soil   you*
> *make a vaulting of*
> *sticks   an extended*
> *tent   the fine tips &*
> *small buds crossing*
> *hands at the top*
>
> *when your peas*
>
> *are planted & you've*
> *waited they'll twine*

> *& creep up both sides*
> *of the tent until they*
> *tangle together at the*
> *top & drop fat pods*
> *into sheltered air*
> *between them &*
> *the ground*

The quarry was a mysterious place, abandoned when I was very young in favour of a new and more productive site to the east of our garden. It was the centre of our boy's-own world. A place we mapped in our minds as clearly and extensively as any ordinance survey map – except our priorities were different. What we had in mind were special places, sites of adventures and tales, bird's nests, haunts of badgers and secret dens. The landscape was part physical, part myth, part memory, part invention. And these parts were equal and intermingled. We moved from fact to fiction and back again in just a few hundred paces of our endless wanderings:

> *Bare feet through hillocks of grass, on rock, in birchbark ash, small fire, sun through windy branches.*

> *Last few hours of this day - no end to change, transformations, variations of leaf and light - soon roofs, walls, cracks in concrete only a few years old, will be dug up and relaid with fresh mix.*

>> *How does broom get its yellow*
>> *from grey rock, dusty soil?*

> *Ghosts rise.   Splintered logs.   Owls nest in my ears, they gaze both ways across night spaces between tree and tree. Shrews parting blades of grass like oak churchdoors.*

> *No rest between clouds of yellow smoke and blueless hills sweating in dusk. Flies with no loss of horizon's speech.*

> *So to the quarry's edge, stars twinkling across its throat.*

> *Rusty old cars, bikes, tin cans, comics flaking every few weeks, mass decreasing - giving themselves to the earth which takes without question.*

The tales were never-ending, erupting out of the rock and bramble:

> *in the yellow field*
>
> *I found a wild goat*
> *with a tattered ear　he'd*
> *caught somehow in a thicket*
> *on a thorn　bitch-of-a-bush*
> *bellowed & threshed dark*
> *under black-pine　came out*
> *red-eared & wet of sweat*
> *& blood　lay down by the mill*
> *licked it dry　& slept*
>
> *I met him perhaps two hours*
> *later　freshly wounded　grey*
> *beard*
> > *one*
> > *snow-ear*

But that was long ago in a land grown radiant with remembered dramas and endless reverie. Now, sitting in the silver-grey red cedar house I look out at a different world, though how I look at it hasn't changed much — I still find an opening to the beauty of it all, a daily rapture at small things, a quiet satisfaction to see so much.

Gazing out at the garden I remember the rain: the hush of it, the steady fall of millions of drops, each containing a version of the world in its lens-like globe, and the sweet fragrance of earth released into the atmosphere by some alchemy of water meeting soil. Sitting on the big log of the fallen turkey oak on a summer's evening, I could feel the weight of wet branches and verdure above me, the downturned arc of each leaf as a raindrop runs its length, down the central vein, pausing at the tip, fattening into a perfectly poised droplet that stretches until its skin can no longer contain it and then falls as the leaf bounces back to its usual position in space - before the next raindrop gathers and the whole cycle happens again. All over the tree and its neighbours leaves are nodding at different rates, a complex rhythmic movement that never loses its fascination. And the sound of this arboreal ballet is a gentle mix of hiss, shuuh and irregular drip, plop, plup and putter. It is the most beautiful evensong imaginable and seems to wash away all the dust that coats my skin and my senses, dispelling all thoughts that hang heavy at the end of a day, leaving only clarity and lightness.

One autumn afternoon I watched the falling leaves and the tender fading light:

> *walking in the quiet shoals of*
> *trees dropping gold, finding*
> *what was never lost, slowly*
> *turning each leaf to dream*
> *as if it had never been,*
>
>   *yet*
>
> *I see each nibbled edge and,*
> *even now, can smell the puzzling*
> *scent of fibre mixed with bone*
>
> *in the quiet shoals, dreams are*
> *scattered, scenting the air with*
> *the labour of resurrection,*
> *pillowing the way for rosaries*
> *of fungus and plainsong of*
> *hallowed microbes*

Once, just after dawn, I walked up into the wood and found a roe deer lying dead near the path. Its stomach had been torn open, probably by a fox. Perhaps I'd disturbed the fox at the beginning of a good eat. The deer must have been weakened by illness, maybe it had just died and the fox had found it as I did – a bounty for old Reynard, a burial task for me. I dragged the heavy carcass, its limbs and neck still supple, into a shaded place under a holly bush. I moved a pile of cut branches, dug a large hole to the depth of my knees and curled the deer's body into the cavity. As I tossed in the first few spadefuls of earth I found myself asking for peace for the deer and thinking of it wandering up from the valley the previous evening or during the night. It must have crossed a few gardens and a lane to get here. Perhaps it had been here before, on one of its forays for food.

Interwoven Nature

Perhaps it remembered the small wood with its high fence on one side and a few gaps to get in. Maybe it was drawn to the relative security of this space as a place to rest and wait for what was to come, knowing that nearby there were flowers and lettuces to eat should the morning bring a healing. I covered the grave with leafmould and replaced the tangle of cut branches to hide and protect it. A few months later I found a fox dead from no apparent injuries, only a few yards from where I'd found the deer. I buried it under another holly, covering it with a broken piece of fencing. The two bodies, two feet deep, lie on an axis from southwest to northeast. I think of the fox when the bitter winter winds blow, and the deer when the fearsome southwesterlies bring mild air and rain. Both winds hardly move the low branches of the two holly bushes under which the bones of the long-dead rest like pale wands in the darkness.

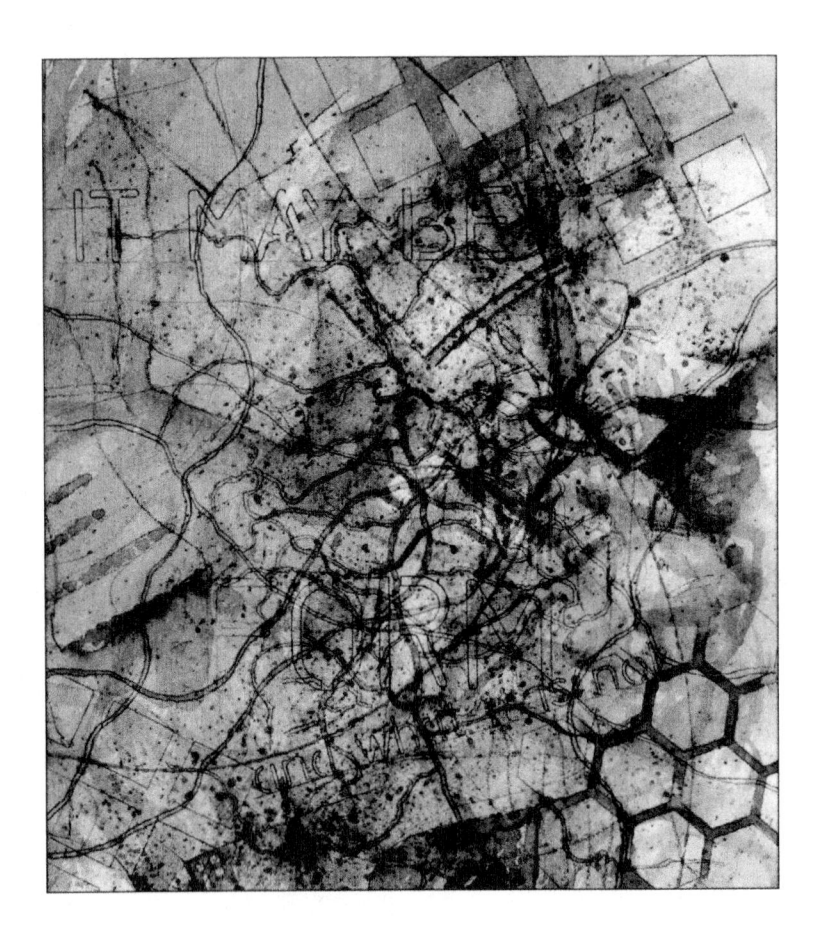

The old man remembers and ponders

Was it Bede who wrote:

> *For no man thinks*
> *more than he need,*
> *of where he is going*
> *and what he will meet?*

We never know what is to come, what winds will blow, from which direction and whether they will bring good or ill.

90 Interwoven Nature

VIII. BUDDHISM, DAOISM, SHAMANISM AND NATURE

Buddhism can be seen as a body of ideas and practices aimed at enabling anyone to become fully awake – to become aware of what it is to be here, to be alive at this moment. In the Zen tradition to sit in meditation is to treat all phenomena as being of equal importance, to be experienced and observed with equal care, acuity and equanimity. There is no thought, sensation or feeling that is too mundane or too small to be unworthy of mindful attention. Awakening in this context is to notice without commentary everything that arises, to attend to the interwoven streams of sensations, narratives, images and emotions that constitute consciousness – and to let go of these phenomena as they arise, rather than to try to cling on to them. It is this reciprocal process of attending and letting-go which helps develop a new way of being-in-the-world. In doing so we notice that there are no solid and fixed boundaries to our selves. Instead we notice that we are a constantly changing hub of relationships with everything that surrounds us, humming with information-processing and imaginative construction. We make ourselves from moment to moment, fashioning ourselves out of the materials of our experiences.

According to Stephen Batchelor, the self is 'a project to be realised' rather than a transcendent entity with a fixed essence.[1] We revise our selves from moment to moment, much as a jazz singer improvises a song out of the raw materials of vocal sound. The self we make in this way is a functioning responsive imaginative self that participates in the world and is inseparable from it. The Buddha's teachings are a recipe for action rather than a catalogue of dogmas or rules. He acts as a guide and navigator, helping anyone to enquire into the processes of living in order to re-orient and revise who, and how, we are in the world. And a crucial starting point for this enquiry and re-visioning is the activity of attending without clinging to the stream of sensations, thoughts and feelings that constitute the fluid materials of our self-making. In this sense we are an open work, a work in progress, never finished, never complete.

This process of attending to what goes on inside, around and through us, with care and precision, includes attending without clinging to suffering in all its aspects (from mild dissatisfaction to severe pain and illness) – attending to, and letting go of, the immediate felt pain and to the responses to that pain, the fear and anxiety that can exacerbate the pain itself. To pay attention and let go of the whole spectrum of dissatisfaction, unease and dis-ease can have a profoundly calming effect on the restlessness and confusion we all feel from time to time, enabling us to experience a more peaceful equilibrium in the face of the difficulties of living. Attending to unease also leads to a growing awareness that there is no clear boundary to the self. Our unease is the product of many forces that flow around and through us. We are inextricably linked to the world around us and to other beings, and our dissatisfactions often arise because we forget that we are *not* separate from the world, we forget that we are intertwined with myriad currents of being. By paying attention to what seems like *our* unease and pain, we tend to develop a deeper awareness of the suffering of other beings, which, in turn, gives rise to empathy and compassion, a sense of kinship and connectedness with all beings.

Dogen, (1200-1253) the thirteenth century Japanese Zen teacher, considers the embodied mind to be an integrated whole, denoted by one term, *shin-jin* (body-mind), but he also recognises no essential separation between *shin-jin*, and the world. Hence, Dogen's reference to the ancient Buddhist belief that, 'the entire universe is the true human body. The entire universe is the gate of liberation'.[2] For Dogen, the world and body-mind are co-dependent and permeable. There is no fixed boundary between them. The body-mind is interwoven with the entire universe. The body-mind is a porous field of interpenetrating forces, a mingling of currents of being and awakening, a boundless site or clearing in which realisation can occur.

Embodied minds always exist in a context, at a point in the relational field. We exist at the confluence of many currents of language, culture, chemistry, genetic coding and evolutionary process. We are always sited somewhere. We inhabit a space, a clearing in the universe. Or, as Nichiren Daishonin puts it: 'Environment is like the shadow, and life, the body. Without the body there can be no shadow'.[3] Self and environment are not separate entities. My skin is also the skin of the world – a shared porous membrane through which flow light, oxygen, food, water, sound (and other microscopic beings). In Nichiren Buddhism this idea of mutuality is encapsulated in the term: *esho funi*. *Esho* is a contraction of the Japanese words, *eho* and *shoho*, meaning 'environment' or 'objective world', and 'living self' or 'subjective self'. And *funi* is a contraction of *nini-funi*, meaning 'two but not two', and *funi-nini*, 'not two but two'. We might translate *esho funi* more loosely as 'being-in-the-world' or 'being-here'.[4]

In a poem entitled, Turtle Head Stupa, Musō Soseki (Rinzai School, 1275-1319) evokes this transparency and intermingling of self and world. He writes:

> Now the doors and windows
>   are all open
>   and nothing inside is hidden
> Dharma worlds
>   beyond number
>   are there for you to see.[5]

This verse brings to mind another by Han-shan (translated by Snyder 2000: 525) in which the poet likens himself to a house. Cold Mountain is a translation of Han-shan's own name:

> Cold Mountain is a house
> Without beams or walls.
> The six doors left and right are open
> The hall is blue sky.

> The rooms all vacant and vague
> The east wall beats on the west wall
> At the centre nothing.[6]

*

Kodo Sawaki, a twentieth century Zen teacher writes about *zazen*, sitting meditation: 'Zazen is the way through which you can connect with the whole universe.'[7] Connecting to the universe involves setting aside the conditional or discriminating self to see things as they are in their infinite inter-dependence – this is to be free, to realise natural wisdom – to be wholly here. According to Sawaki when we realise true selfhood in all its transparency 'there is no gap between the true self and all sentient beings'.[8] And as there is no gap between beings, all beings are integral to 'my' being, a facet of the transparent or permeable self. As Uchiyama puts it:

> everything I encounter here and now is a part of my life, I shouldn't treat anything [or anyone, or any being] roughly. I should take care of everything wholeheartedly. I practice in this way. Everything I encounter is my life.[9]

*

Throughout this book I've been trying to suggest that we are participants in the mutuality of existence, embodied manifestations of the chemical, biological and cultural processes that constitute the world we inhabit. I've suggested that there are no 'things' in the world, in the sense of objects with separate fixed essences. What we call 'objects' and 'things', or apples, or beings like mosquitoes and humans, are only conventional labels for states of relationship and interdependence. The skin of the apple, or 'my' skin, is as much the skin of the surrounding space. Merleau-Ponty uses the term 'the flesh of the world' to refer to this zone of contact between us and the world – the fusion of skin and air, eye and light, tongue and food – our reciprocal relationship with our surroundings.[10] At the sub-atomic level there is no separation between apple, skin and the rest of the world. All 'things' are permeable and in flux. We are all endlessly exchanging energies with everything that is around us. We are transparent vessels through which pass waves of sound, cosmic radiation and light. There is no clear boundary between inside and outside. But most of the time we think and act as if there is.

How

>how bees spin
>honeycombs of flight in
>languid air
>
>how blackbirds sculpt
>shafts of song
>
>how rains fall in
>gravity's quiet
>
>how grasses overcome
>the brittleness of
>ice
>
>how *this* is always
>not what it seems
>
>how everything becomes
>something else

A question: where does my mind end and yours begin? I say something or show you something. You listen and look and think about what you've heard and seen. Your thinking extends my thinking, mine yours. When we exchange 'ideas' we are not exchanging *things*, we are involved in a much more complex process of opening out, unfolding and interacting – a process in which our *apparent* boundaries of mind and self are dissolved as we converse, communicate, interpret and reflect. We are mutually active. A mingling of minds happens - thoughts and feelings flow in the space between us, in a liminal zone which is neither mine nor yours but *ours*. It is in this zone that ideas arise and it is for this reason that ideas tend not to be easily bounded by claims of ownership or identity.

*

The arts can be considered as manifestations of this liminal field, of this intermingling of minds we also refer to as culture. Art and poetry can open up the realm of interrelatedness through the use of metaphor, analogy, imagination and association. The arts, like the sciences, can help us to gain a more durable, sustainable understanding of kinship, grounded in a multi-perspectival view, a gathering of learnings from all quarters, from many minds and from many modes of being. Cultural diversity across all life forms can be considered to be as important as biological and chemical diversity – such diversity acts as a resource-base, a bank of potential ways of knowing, doing and being. An important part of that 'resource base' is the polyphony of cultures and languages, human and non-human, which speaks to us *of* ourselves and *about* the world we inhabit.

The world is a hubbub of languages, of songs and stories, dances and images, woven into the air and waters, inscribed on the land, reaching into the past and the future – including the symbol structures and communication systems not only of humans but of other mammals, and of insects and birds, and the information-processing and sharing systems of other organisms. It is in a spirit of embeddedness and participation *in* the universe, that we need to listen to *all* voices – not just our own species, but also the voices of birds, insects, other mammals, trees, flowers, clouds, rivers and mountains – the complex communication systems that hum, vibrate and shimmer throughout the universe. It may be that we think we are speaking metaphorically or poetically when we say that plants talk to each other – but recent studies in plant interactions demonstrate that plants *do* communicate, sharing information about resources and dangers to their well-being. Plants listen to the 'chemical chatter' of their neighbourhood species and participate in a 'social network' via their root systems – the 'rhizosphere'.[11] Mindful meditation (see Chapter XIV), like ecology, is a way of listening, a way of attending to this ceaseless multi-sensory music. And there is no composer or conductor controlling what happens, only an endless process of polyphonic improvisation. For this is a universe at play: purposeless in its entirety, yet made up of countless threads of purpose; without beginning or end, yet made up of countless beginnings and endings – a dynamic relational field of beings and currents of existence. Intuitive understandings of these reciprocal flows of language can be found in the oral poetry of many tribal cultures. Here's an example from the Inuit people of the arctic region, who describe a time, long ago, when:

> The human mind had mysterious powers.
> A word spoken by chance
> might have strange consequences.
> It would suddenly come alive
> and what people wanted to happen could happen –
> all you had to do was say it.
> Nobody could explain this:
> That's the way it was.[12]

As I've already mentioned a useful metaphor for this intermingling of minds and of chemical and biological processes may be the mycelium of a fungus: the mass of thread-like filaments that exist below the ground through which the fungus absorbs and processes nutrients. Mycelia often spread over large areas – cultural networks that interconnect and interweave with each other.

*

This brings us once again to shamanism - an ancient tradition that offers us a model for a way of being-in-the-world that is strikingly ecological. According to David Abram, the purpose of shamanic practices is to establish experiential contact with the non-human realm - developing an ecological awareness grounded in human perception. Abram writes:

> 'Magic, then, in its… most primordial sense, is the experience of existing in a world made up of multiple intelligences, the intuition that every form one perceives… is an experiencing form…'[13]

The idea that there are more intelligences at work in the world than just the human and that these intelligences fill the world with communication systems, codes, stories and songs is a very powerful one – and it is a central belief of many indigenous cultures around the world – and still has relevance insofar as it engenders a reverence for the natural world and its processes and mysteries. Mary Oliver, in her poem, *Sleeping in the Forest*, articulates this idea in her own quiet voice:

> …I slept
> as never before, a stone
> on the riverbed, nothing
> between me and the white fire of the stars
> but my thoughts, and they floated
> light as moths among the branches
> of the perfect trees. All night
> I heard the small kingdoms breathing
> around me, the insects, and the birds
> who do their work in the darkness…[14]

In this kind of writing a balance has to be struck between anthropocentric personalisation and empathic imagining. The danger is always that nature becomes too domesticated, too soft and furry. R.S.Thomas offers an antidote to a cosy view of nature in the doubled image of a barn owl, which he describes as 'soft / feathers camouflaging a machine' - a machine that 'repeats itself year / after year'.[15] In a similar vein Rexroth reminds us of the indifference of stones, the remoteness of the geosphere, 'the cold and cruel apathy of mountains' – though this image in a different way is anthropocentric - for we can hardly accuse mountains of 'apathy', let alone 'cruelty'.[16]

*

Zen teacher Dogen (1200-1253) reminds us of one of the most important insights of the Buddha: 'Delusion is seeing all things from the perspective of the self. Enlightenment is seeing the self from the perspective of the myriad things of the universe'.[17] We could put this slightly differently: we are mistaken if we believe and act as if each ego/self is a fixed and essential centre of the universe; we become wise when we act on the belief that the self has no fixed essence and is woven into the universe and inseparable from it. If we believe in an essential self, separated from the rest of the world, we think we act in our own self-interest by trying to satisfy every desire of our ego, and our politics, culture and social organisation reflect this need for self-fulfilment, at the expense of all other considerations. Yet, as Peter Timmerman points out, 'how can we survive on a planet of [eight] billion points of infinite greed?'[18] This delusory way of living is clearly unsustainable. While ecology provides the analytical tools to understand the interconnectedness of living systems, Buddhism offers an alternative way of being-in-the-world that harmonises with ecological understanding.

When Dogen and other Mahayana Buddhists use the term 'Buddha-nature' they are not referring to an essence or soul or core of being. When we say that all beings manifest Buddha-nature we are acknowledging that insofar as all beings have no fixed essence, soul or Atman, but are instead fluid and transient currents of existence within an infinite relational field, then *all* beings are as open to, and as likely to be agents of, enlightenment as the Buddha. Human nature, seen from this perspective, is a manifestation of all of nature – as we see the world reflected in an infinite variety of ways in every raindrop that falls, as every illuminated surface in a dancehall is reflected in the rotating mirrored globe which, in its turn, casts its reflections on every surface.

Each of us is a community of organisms, cells and atoms – which is why taking a community perspective, an ecological viewpoint, makes so much sense and why the maintenance of bio-diversity and cultural diversity is crucial to our well-being. It has been recently proposed that we have now entered (possibly beginning in the industrial revolution) a new era in planetary evolution: the Anthropocene period. An era marked by the impact upon the earth of one species: Homo sapiens – human beings. Certainly there are few places on earth that aren't affected by human activities. Large areas of the globe are habitats managed by humans – in the form of agriculture, horticulture, mineral extraction and urban expansion. We have to take full responsibility for these managed habitats and consider carefully what we do as individuals acting within, and on behalf of, diverse communities of beings.

Considered in this way we have to accept that states with a large Buddhist presence have often been no less harmful to the environment than have non-Buddhist communities. Deforestation, industrial degradation and, in many cases, intolerance of minorities and lack of care for other species, is as widespread in China, Japan, Thailand, Myanmar and Korea as it is in ostensibly Christian or Islamic countries. We need to think of Buddhist temples and monasteries as managed habitats in the same way that we consider domestic gardens, allotments and farmland as sites in which many interwoven communities live. The more diverse are these communities and the more attuned they are to local conditions the more sustainable they are in the long run. A Zen dry garden, though on a small scale, could be seen as being as barren and ecologically unsound as a soil-depleted mono-crop intensive farm in the American Midwest! Maybe we need to treat *every acre of land as a sacred site*, as first and foremost *a home* – only in this way might we restore the planet to health.

For the Buddha, Dogen, Kodo Sawaki and Nichiren Daishonin there are no firm boundaries between things and therefore we are intimately related to everything else. Coming to this realisation and understanding that our being extends into our surroundings leads to a sense of participation and kinship that underpins the Buddhist beliefs in compassion, minimising harm done to others and in 'loving-kindness' towards all of creation. Although our ability to translate these beliefs into action is always limited by historical understanding and cultural conditioning, in the twenty-first century we are in a position to extend Buddhist compassion, not only to our fellow humans but to our kith and kin throughout the natural world – from mice to mountains, from tiny bacteria to vast river systems – to listen to the songs sung by every organism and to learn from all beings. It is this shift of viewpoint – from the one to the many, the part to the whole – that Buddhism, and ecology in a very different way, work towards – providing us with tools and methods that enable us to experience the world as it is, to come to a realisation of who, and how, we are in the world: to fully realise that we are relational beings in a relational universe.

*

The following well-known poem by e.e.cummings can be seen as drawing together many of the strands of thought I have just been exploring:

> O sweet spontaneous
> earth how often have
> the
> doting
>
>   fingers of
> prurient philosophers pinched
> and
> poked

thee
, has the naughty thumb
of science prodded
thy

    beauty . how
often have religions taken
thee upon their scraggy knees
squeezing and

buffeting thee that thou mightiest conceive
gods
       (but
true
to the incomparable
couch of death thy
rhythmic
lover

    thou answerest

them only with
        spring)[19]

*

Dogen, one of the founders of the Soto school of Japanese Zen Buddhism, argues that to know the self is both to lose the self and to find the self. The found self both is, and is not, the self that is lost. What he points to is that when we examine the self, through mindfulness or bare attention, we encounter a stream of ever-changing processes, a stream of moods, wishes, emotions, thoughts and images. There seems to be no unchanging nucleus, soul or ego – only the river of experiences. In Buddhism, the term *skandhas* denotes this shifting stream of processes (or 'aggregates' as they are often called).

Usually five kinds of *skandha* are described: *rūpa* - the physical world of form and matter; *vedanā* - the sensations and feelings we experience in response to physical stimuli – which may be pleasant, unpleasant or neutral; *samjñā* - the process of sorting, classifying and recognising, by which we perceive an apple as an apple or a table as a table or a person as a person; *samskāra* - the mental formations and forces (desires, impulses and will), and the habits of thought, behaviour and response built up over our lifetime, which drive our actions and mental responses; and, *vijñāna* - the process of being conscious and having awareness – including self-awareness. It is where these currents of causality meet that our sense of self arises. We arise as the five skandhas interact - forming and reforming over time.

If we closely examine our consciousness we notice that we can never pin down the 'I' that is having the experience. Whenever we think we have found the 'I' we find there is yet another 'I' who is doing the finding! It is as if there is no-one behind the counter, no-one standing at the back of the room of consciousness who owns all that happens in the room. Instead there is only a bewildering succession of 'I's, or rather a flickering stream of interconnected moments of consciousness, that, like frames in a reel of film give rise to a believable reality when they move at a particular speed and when light is projected through them. Our self is a process, not a 'thing'. Maybe *selfing* is how we should describe the unfolding of our being.

According to Dogen, to realise the true nature of the self is to open 'the gate of liberation' – to be liberated from categorising and dualistic thought. In realising that there are no fixed limits or impermeable boundaries to the self (to conscious being) is to have a transformed sense of who we are and how interwoven we are with everything else. It also means that we recognise that there is no liberation and no gate because the boundless self *is* the universe and the universe is the self!

*

There is an interesting parallel between some of the points I've been making and Daoist ideas about nature, both the nature of the world and human nature. Alan Watts argues that the Dao can be considered as 'the indefinable, concrete 'process' of the world, the Way [*Dao*] of life'.[20] In other words, the Dao is a dynamic undifferentiated field of energy or process that is indefinable and ineffable. It works, according to Daoists by not-working, it makes by not-making, it is a self-organising system and its process is one of growth in which it spontaneously generates forms and entities.[21] This process of acting by not-acting is denoted by the Chinese term, *wu-wei*.[22] Metaphorically, this process is likened to the action of wind and water, to flexibility, fluidity and bending rather than rigidity. And it is the suppleness and indeterminacy of the Dao which stands the test of time, enabling growth to be sustained in its infinite forms.

We can also think of *wu-wei* as non-intention, or as arising not from the nucleic, Cartesian ego but from the *selfless self*. That is, the self as permeable fluid process rather than as an object or essence – the self as one filament within the web of existence. Daoism considers the world and the self as intermingled and co-arising, an ecological perspective which is very different to the anthropocentric or *ego*-centric view.

*

John Dewey (1859-1952), the American pragmatist philosopher, has some interesting things to say on these matters. One of the key features of Dewey's thinking is the importance he attaches to experience and human action, and the way he conceptualises living and experiencing as process. Stephen C. Rockefeller points out that Dewey employs a vocabulary of evolution and growth throughout his writings. As far as Dewey is concerned there is no goal or final destination towards which human beings are progressing. In Rockefeller's words, 'Life is process. The self is process. The end of human life is not to attain some static ideal state and stop growing. The only end of living is to be found in a way of living'.[23]

For Dewey the universe is a relational field, a network of interacting and interdependent processes, constantly changing, constantly evolving. Human beings are agents within this field, weaving narratives and actions into the complex unfolding multi-dimensional tapestry of events. In Dewey's view each entity and each stream of consciousness is unique, acting within the relational field in a distinctive and unrepeatable way. On the other hand each entity only exists as a thread in the web of relationships which constitute the universe. As Rockefeller argues, 'There is real singularity and individuality in nature, but nothing exists as an isolated entity'.[24] This is as true of the human self as it is of a lemon, a cloud or an amoeba. Diversity is integral to Dewey's conception of the universe as an 'infinite complex of interacting events'.[25] Dewey speaks of the 'miscellaneous and uncoordinated plurals of our actual world'[26] – a world of ceaseless motion and interaction, about which we can never reach any conclusions, final answers or definitive theories. All we can do is try to find an effective way of living with this unending mutability.

> No matter where
> we look surprises turn
> assumptions to ash,
> smoke twisting into
> all the shapes we can't
> imagine
>
> I can only
> guess at what this journey
> will bring:

watermeadows
strapped with iris-blades,
meadowsweet sloughing
cream skins in shadows
where oaks lose their fisted
roots

nothing is as we
think it will be
always our expectations
flit like bats
in and out of
what is
and what is
not

---

[1] Batchelor 2010: 152
[2] Tanahashi 1995: 163
[3] in Seymour 1996
[4] *ibid*
[5] in Davidson 2007: 163
[6] translated by Snyder 2000: 525
[7] in Uchiyama 1990: 80
[8] *ibid*: 20
[9] *ibid*: 124
[10] in Abram 1997: 68
[11] see Jabr 2011: 46
[12] Rothenberg 1972: 45
[13] Abram 1997: 9
[14] Oliver 1979: 3
[15] Thomas 2001: 319
[16] Rexroth 2003: 161
[17] Habito 1997: 170
[18] Timmerman 1992: 74
[19] Cummings 1963: 3
[20] Watts 1989: 15
[21] *ibid:* 16-17

[22] *ibid*: 19
[23] Rockefeller 1989: 229
[24] *ibid*: 221
[25] *ibid*: 220
[26] *ibid*: 221

108   Interwoven Nature

IX. THE OLD MAN OBSERVES THE CITY

Over the horizon spiders of war spin their webs – trapping thousands, maybe millions – stuck fast to delicate filaments of distrust, anger, prejudice, fear. It's hard to see the fine tracery until it's too late.

I see a shaking leaf in a shimmering desert and I fall into poverty, great hardship, dreams and torments. I am imprisoned by despair for all the hurt that courses through every living creature. In this lowly state I am cornered in nakedness while angels gather amongst trees casting a golden flickering at my feet, washing my skin with a cool darkness that turns my small griefs to ash and gentle steam.

I once met a man who said he had slept with wolves. Another who claimed to have heard the ancient music of stones. Yet another who suggested he had spent his days among lepers, searching for a silver cloud. Elijah, who had stone feet, followed a path of stones in a landscape of stones under a stone sky. Someone told me that John the Baptist's coat was woven out of the hides of camels, held close to his body by a frayed rope thrown away by a shepherd. He slept on the ground in raging heat and numbing cold. He drank only morning dew and ate seeds, honey and locusts. When he described his God he seemed to speak nonsense, or not to speak at all, for his listeners only heard a vocabulary of tattered moans and murmurs, torn sounds and sacred syllables that defied rational explanation. He seemed to utter a holy mumble: aar ata, hut u tum, umma umma ha.... At each river he became a white light veiled in skin. He taught wild dogs to fly and birds to howl. None of the people whom he baptised could remember their names. He never tired of giving them new ones.

I remember sitting in the big museum overcome by the sheer quantity of it all. All the scripts and signs of the world seemed to be there, pointing and crying out to be heard. Each broken tile and shard of pot spoke of hands and minds toiling to be remembered if not to be understood. Curves of clay, bronze, gold, wood and stone echoed the play of hands on a lover's limbs and the play of light on a lover's face. I could only catch a glimpse of such love and tenderness, faint starlight of worlds long gone yet still flickering in glass cabinets. Around me was the pain of desiring and losing, making and undoing, dreaming and forgetting. Everywhere I could see catalogues of love and loss, archives of touch and glance.

Every time I catch a glimpse of myself and my world in a mirror I'm reminded of the fact that I will never again see this reflection, never again see this old coat draped over the chair or these cracked teacups turned upsidedown or the spectacles' case empty on the bed. Never again will I hear the barking of small dogs in Aberdeen. I'll never again remember the ferry ride across the river in Brisbane or look on the face of the black bear on the other side of Ribbon Creek. I will never again hear this robin singing at dawn or the cockerel crowing, or see the faint light through this thin curtain. I'll never again see that shadow below the plum tree or that one beneath the red car or that one beneath the woman's arm.

In Spencer's translation, Joachim de Bellay writes of Rome:

> *That which is firm doth flit & fall away,*
> *And that is flitting, doth abide & stay.*[1]

We write to say hello to the world, and to say goodbye – to share what has happened to us, to sing ourselves into another kind of being. Our thoughts are inscribed on the awkward surfaces of the world. It is as if we wanted to bind ourselves to what surrounds us, to weave ourselves into every nook and cranny of what we see, taste, hear, smell and touch. There is nothing that is not filled with our presence. Yet though we are everywhere, we are nowhere. There is no centre that holds our mind, no nucleus to our being. We flit and fall away, yet we abide. Like plankton we are mingled and dispersed, carried with currents that are not of our making, emerging and merging we span a territory far beyond our skin.

There is so much turmoil in human affairs. We tie ourselves to contradictory beliefs and arbitrary judgements as if they were absolutes cast in concrete. We are full of self-righteous anger at those who do not see things as we do. And yet at other times we help those who have fallen on hard times, even if they speak a different language and have different beliefs. We fail to take the buzzard's view: looking down on the world he sees men rushing here and there, scurrying from place to place, belief to belief, posture to posture. But from his high winged throne he can see why they rush about, what they run from and towards, the reasons for their actions. This gives him a wisdom that they do not have. He can see that the causes are always changing, the circumstances ebbing and flowing in a way that is unpredictable and complicated. Human affairs are a bramble patch of barbed and tangled threads, enmeshing us in contortions, rages, blindnesses and delusions. But the buzzard sees all of this. We should learn from the buzzard, as we should from the mole snug in his darkness, or the cricket chirping his way through the swaying grasses. It makes me think again of the Wanderer, who writes:

> 'There is so much trouble in our human world;
> we are pushed and jostled by the fates.
> Wealth is short-lived, friends come and go,
> we are temporary, our lovers are soon gone,
> there is nothing upon which we can rely.'
> So said the wise man who sat apart in meditation.[2]

The buzzard and the wise man stand aloof only insofar as they are cautious in their judgements. They look for causes and circumstances. They wait to see how events unfold before they make up their minds and even then they hold themselves ready to change their views. As the Wanderer says:

> A wise man should be patient, and hold back his anger,
> he should not be too hasty in speaking,
> nor too reckless, greedy or boastful.
> He needs to know all sides of an argument
> before speaking, criticising or praising.[3]

*

When I look down into the valley the sea is a distant and delicate change of tone beneath the broad grey sky. The city is sometimes enveloped in mist and only the spires of churches and the square towers of the cathedral jut out like exclamation marks. On the streets and in the shops, pubs and clubs people gather to barter ideas, to buy and sell goods, to eat, dance and drink. They are drawn together by some force that ensnares them as securely as the ties of love or hate. And here they build unsteady constructions of community and collective dreaming, wrapping themselves in each other's stories until they find it hard to see the living world at the city's edge. Enmeshed in images of themselves, their desires and passions

112 Interwoven Nature

inscribed on billboards, in shop windows, on tv and in the mycelia of social networks, the citizens lose touch with physical things. They become like ghosts removed from their surroundings, no longer hearing the calls of birds or seeing the night foxes padding across the car parks or the rose-cheeked clouds passing overhead on a spring morning. Their world is circumscribed by a fog of self-generating needs, habits, envies and obsessions. Even illness and death come as a shock, a disruption to the order of things, rather than an inevitability to be prepared for and reflected upon. Shoppers pursue bargains that are forgotten as soon as they are purchased, tokens of desires that can never be satisfied. And secluded in glittering glasshouses bankers and speculators juggle numbers and tend their computing machines, piling up a frothy confection of vapid wealth and gossamer-thin success. In the gambling dens of finance feverish men contemplate chains of debt that no-one seems to understand or be able to follow back to their source in actual coins or notes. In this ethereal realm of high finance, where phantoms converse with phantoms, nothing is produced other than another IOU or another bundle of stocks and shares. No-one makes anything of substance or beauty or use. Instead, wealth is pursued with every throw of the dice and the world of touch and taste and living tissue is a remote and alien sphere. The link between earth and enduring wealth has been lost........

[1] From the poem, *Antiquitez de Rome*, in Pinter et al, 1994: 21
[2] This seems to be the old man's rendition of lines 101-106 from *The Wanderer* elegy in 'The Exeter Book' – probably based on the Michelle Blair translation.
[3] Perhaps this is his garbled version of lines 62-66 of the same text.

114   Interwoven Nature

X. THE ART OF EVERYDAY LIVING

> 'Glory be to God for dappled things –
> For skies of couple-colour as a brinded cow;
> For rose-moles all in stipple upon trout that swim;
> Fresh-firecoal chestnut-falls; ....'[1]

In this chapter I would like to discuss a particular aspect of our being-in-the-world: the way in which *being here* can be considered as a creative activity, a creative engagement with the world in which we live alongside a seemingly infinite variety of other forms of life. If approached in a creative way, as an art, our day-to-day existence can be a source of endless surprise and interest, and if we develop the art of everyday living even the most humdrum and mundane of events and things can be transformed into objects of beauty, wonder and fascination. Seen from such a perspective everyday living is a creative process and *this* world is a place of unending mystery, open to infinite avenues of enquiry and celebration.

*

It will be useful to begin by considering the notion of creativity itself, questioning some of the widely-held views about creativity as a special attribute of gifted individuals, an attribute that is not shared by everyone. I'd like to challenge this view by suggesting that there is nothing special about creativity. Indeed creativity is unavoidable, as unavoidable as breathing or sensing.

Each moment of consciousness is a creative moment, a manifestation of the infinite creativity of living and being. What artists do is only one of the multiple forms of creativity, a practice amongst countless creative practices – and these practices range from raising a child to running a business, gardening to plumbing, testing out a theory in a laboratory to sweeping the backyard, painting a wall to painting a portrait, writing a letter to writing a poem.... these are all manifestations of creative thinking and doing within the human realm.

And on what grounds are we not to include the creativity of other species and natural forms? The blackbird singing endless melodic variations from his perch on the crab apple tree, the bees at work in and around the hive, ants 'milking' greenfly for their honeydew, chimpanzees sucking termites from the end of a stick they've probed into a mound – they're all exercising powers of invention and adaptability. And what about the less obvious creative practices of clouds, endlessly performing subtle or dramatic cloud dances, or the pizzicato mutterings of mountain streams, or the stately, centuries long, growth of lichen on a Dartmoor boulder? Are there any boundaries between patterns of growth and decay in the natural world and the patterns of creative intelligence manifested in the growth of human imaginative constructs? I suspect there are no clear-cut distinctions to be made, unless we consider creativity to be defined by purposeful self-consciousness – in which case the zone of creative practice shrinks to a narrow and greatly-diminished sphere of activity.

*

We use the term creativity to refer to many different qualities and doings. It is often used to denote distinctive ways of being, thinking and making that demonstrate flexibility, innovation, inventiveness and the confounding of expectations and assumptions. Intuition, improvisation and non-linear ways of thinking are often emphasized, as are, experiment, trying-things-out, making a mess, working productively with high levels of disorder, uncertainty & indeterminacy. Elements of chance and serendipity are often essential – both in the creative process and in the products of creativity. And there's often an element of spontaneity and of being surprised by what emerges. A sense of something unexpected, not predetermined.

From a Buddhist perspective creativity can be enhanced by the development of an open non-discriminatory mode of awareness – 'mindfulness' – a disinterested attention to all that arises – a non-centred awareness. In this way the creative stream of human being can flow, unimpeded by the desires and demands of the deluded self.

*

There is a widespread belief that creativity is associated with specialness, creativity as a distinctive characteristic of a few individuals - artistic and poetic 'geniuses' - whose actions and utterances are seen as being of a different (and superior) order to that of ordinary folk. Vasari paved the way for this break between the creative domain and the domain of the rest of us, when he began to write of Renaissance artists as eccentric individuals with special and unusual gifts. Vasari saw this as evidence of human beings exhibiting God-like powers. Indeed he argued that Michelangelo had been sent by God in order to show others how to 'attain perfection in design'.[2] Evidence of divine intervention, of creativity as a 'gift' bestowed on a few rather than as an innate attribute of all, becomes part of the cultural sediment of the 19th Century and is canonised in 20th Century Modernism.

In this account creativity becomes the prerogative of artists, composers, poets and, occasionally, distinguished 'men of science'. Blake's image of Isaac Newton executing the geometry of God on an earthly surface embodies this view. Leonardo becomes the epitome of polymathic creativity, and Picasso is accorded the status of a demi-god - the icon of masculine virility and creative energy. The patriarchical power-base at the centre of this view is obvious. As is the rhetoric of fertility: 'giving birth to ideas and images'; artworks as the 'offspring or children' of male artists; 'fecundity of ideas'; etc. - all assuming an association between cultural production and biological reproduction, or, alternatively, male envy, fear or arrogance enshrined in the robust exercising of creative power.

However this view of creativity can be contrasted with the ideas of artists like John Cage, Yoko Ono, Joseph Beuys and Marina Abramovic, and philosophical thinkers like Ruskin, Merleau-Ponty,

Howard Gardner and John Dewey, as well as many proponents of Buddhist thought and practice. In all of these sources we encounter a view of creativity as an integral part of our make-up as human beings. Creative thought and action are characteristics of our being in the world, dynamic attributes of our perceptual and conceptual systems. This poses a democratised challenge to the other elitist and restrictive view.

The Romantic/Modernist tradition considers creativity as both unteachable and as the genetic endowment of a few individuals: some people are creative, others aren't – you've either got the 'gift' or you haven't. On the other hand the counter-tradition I've described sees creativity as a fundamental capacity or potential of everyone – something that can be encouraged and nurtured and learned. Indeed learning itself can be seen as quintessentially creative.

*

The French philosopher, Merleau-Ponty, argues that perception is itself a creative process by which we encounter, handle and make sense of the world of things and other beings. Perceiving the most insignificant object, involves a complex and creative encounter with the world. We are knowing bodies implicated *in* the world, not separate from it. Merleau-Ponty also suggests that we build our *selves* in a continuous stream of creative acts which forge our distinctive identity. We make who we are in each of our thoughts, perceptions and actions, and in our interactions with others and the world. Buddhist practice adds to, or subtracts from, this idea, the realisation (sudden or slow) that the 'self' is, in a sense, a fiction, a social construction, without any fixed or unitary essence. Recognising that we need not be defined and confined by an apparently enduring self, we can learn to let go, to change, to move from state to state, to be creative and to creatively be! By shifting our frame of reference we realise that the self is a ceaseless creative dance of embodied mind, constantly unfolding into new possibilities and potentialities. Through disciplined learning practices we can come to realise that the self is a dynamic creative process rather than a fixed entity.

These thoughts on selfhood can lead us to question the notion that we 'have' ideas. What is it to have an idea? Should it be the other way around - are we 'had' by ideas? Do we inhabit ideas, or are we inhabited by them? And who is it who 'has' the idea?

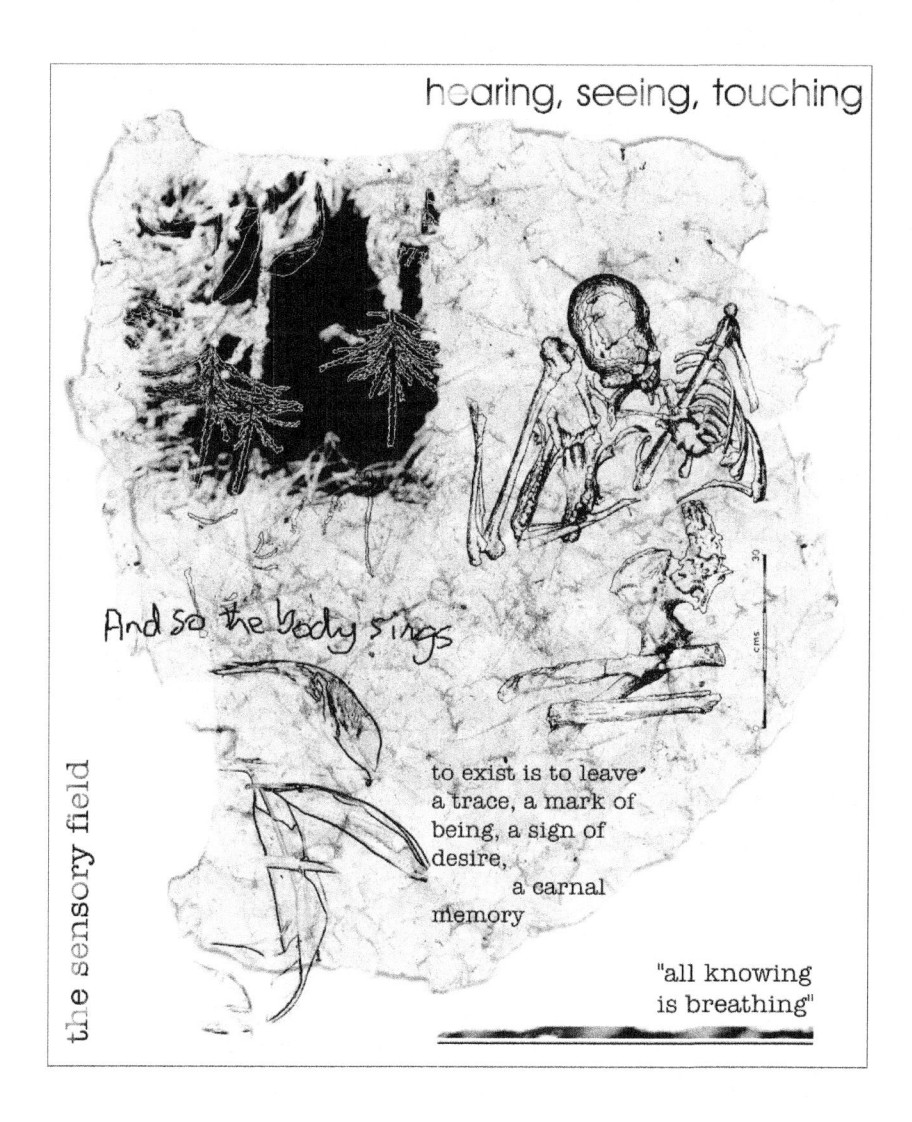

> hearing, seeing, touching
>
> And so the body sings
>
> the sensory field
>
> to exist is to leave
> a trace, a mark of
> being, a sign of
> desire,
>   a carnal
>   memory
>
> "all knowing
> is breathing"

An idea arises as a moment of consciousness. The more we relax our hold on the linguistic or conceptualising self the more likely it is that ideas will arise out of the flux of interactions deep in the neurological system. Being in possessive mode in relation to ideas can be counter-productive. In a sense the less we try to 'have' ideas the more likely it is that they will arise. Getting our 'selves' out of the picture may unlock the flow of creative neurological activity.

Experiential evidence from the sciences and the arts points to the effectiveness of 'letting go', even of 'giving up', allowing the intuitive, pre-linguistic processes to run 'underground' in the mind – at the margins of consciousness rather than at the centre of attention. In these conditions ideas often emerge in 'Eureka'- mode. The Daoist phrase, *wu-wei*, 'doing by not-doing' seems appropriate - letting things happen of their own accord.

*

Meister Eckhart suggests that: 'Art is an act of attention, not of will' – a phrase that was often quoted by the composer, John Cage.

*

The seventeenth-century Rinzai Zen master, Bankei, (1622-93, also known as Kokushi) turns the popular notion of creativity on its head. He centres his teaching on what had been for centuries a key Buddhist term in Japan, *Fu-sho*, 'the Unborn', or Buddha-mind or Buddha-nature: that which is 'intrinsic, original and *uncreated*'.[3] Bankei tells us that to *be* truly alive we need only recognise with all of our being that we *are* truly alive. The state of enlightenment, liberation or peace that human beings so frantically crave, is only to be realised by letting-go of the craving – which is built on illusion and mis-understanding. Similarly creativity, which is a manifestation of being truly alive, is not something that needs to be learnt or *added* to our being, rather it is a way of being that is most immediate and ready-at-hand, often realised by unlearning, unknowing, letting-go. Paradoxically, the process of realising by letting-go may require a very systematic discipline: the discipline of the *koan*; of Madhyamika dialectics; of ascetic routines and highly-organised periods of meditation; or the discipline of drawing a stone over and over again in order to see the stone as if for the first time – what Lawrence

Weschler refers to with the phrase, 'seeing is forgetting the name of the thing one sees'.[4]

*

While creativity is usually lauded as 'a good thing', a quality always to be nurtured, it is important to keep in mind that creativity is not ethically neutral, let alone universally 'good'. Sadly, human beings are as creative in the arts of war, cruelty and repression as they are in the arts of peace, care, tolerance and liberation. Creativity can be a force for good, a way to, and a manifestation of, enlightenment and liberation, but it can also be a force for domination, selfishness and exploitation. The way in which creativity is manifested and exercised defines its moral value, though paradoxically, as already mentioned, there is a kind of purposelessness or playfulness that seems integral to creativity.

*

The highest we can aspire to is the ordinary, the everyday, the humdrum – the art, or creative practice, of living. Attending, without clinging, to the stream of everyday experiences is a profound creative activity. Sawaki Roshi points out: 'Everyday life has rainy days, windy days, and stormy days. So you can't always be happy. It's the same with *zazen*.'[5] Uchiyama adds that Zen meditation is at heart 'the practice of continuous awareness in the midst of delusion, without attachment to delusion or enlightenment.'[6] In a similar vein Georges Dreyfus suggests, the everyday sound of *two* hands clapping may, in the end, be more important (and creative) than the rare sound of *one* hand clapping.[7]

Speaking very much in the tradition of Dogen and Bankei, Sawaki Roshi de-mythologizes and debunks the notion that *satori* or enlightenment are extraordinary or special attainments. At one point he goes so far as to say: 'there is no way to fail in becoming a Buddha [.....] The night train carries you along even when you are sleeping.'[8] He suggests that however we may clothe *satori* or enlightenment in special properties, there is in actuality nothing special about realising Buddha-nature – it is to be just as we are, no less and no more. The view of Buddha Mind as special is delusive in that it depends on attachment to the idea of specialness, it is to sit in meditation *in order to become* special (enlightened). It is to sit, polishing the tile of the self in the hope that it will become a mirror of enlightenment – but, as Nangaku (in Chinese, Nan-yüeh)[9] and Dogen, in the *Fukanzazengi*, argue, it never does. Sawaki's gentle critique of the tendency to mythologize or Romanticise Buddha Mind, can be applied to the tendency to Romanticise creative practice in relation to the arts – to diminish creativity by associating it only with genius. Paradoxically, as Dogen points out, if we polish the tile *for its own sake*, with no thought of reward, we may well realise Buddha Mind.[10]

*

Another aspect of creativity that is often neglected is the ability to make connections. We often think of creativity in terms of originality, making something out of nothing. But of course, all that comes out of nothing, is nothing. A pile of zeros is still zero. We always need material out of which to make something, whether it's paint, bricks, flour or thought. Often creativity involves connecting something to something else, in a new or surprising way. Making connections, or noticing connections, is itself a creative act, and to notice connections is to *be* connected, to experience the interrelationship and interdependence of all that exists. The feeling of interconnectedness is also often accompanied by a feeling of compassion.

*

Sekkei Harada makes reference to the famous *koan* in which: 'Joshu asked his master, Nansen, "What is the Way?" – that is, 'what is the Way of the Buddha'. Nansen replied, "Everyday mind is the Way"'.[11]

Harada suggests that: 'The words "everyday mind" express the condition of our lives free of our own ideas and opinions. Washing one's face, brushing one's teeth, talking, taking meals, working – all these activities [can] take place before thought'.[12] That is, before we weave our chattering mind around them – adding layers of commentary and feeling to the activities themselves. Everyday actions are an actualisation of Buddha Mind if we don't cling to them or add unnecessary layers of hopes, intentions, worries and expectations to them.

This accords with Dogen's emphasis in the '*Genjokoan*', on the activities of daily life - full of ups and downs, routines and seeming mundanity - as a continuation of the formal *koans* encountered in the temple context. For Dogen there are countless ways in which we can realise our Buddha-nature and countless modes of expression and communication through which we can manifest Buddha-mind – these range from verbal teachings and stories to the way in which we do things (for instance, walking, sitting, cooking), even the way in which we stand in a room. Indeed, Dogen shares with Jacob Boehme, a belief that the world and everything in it is a manifestation of cosmic creativity, an expression of what Dogen calls Buddha-mind or Buddha-nature, and Boehme calls God or *Ungrund*.[13]

*

One of the many difficulties of the apparently simple act of *zazen*, sitting meditation, is to be aware of the endless stream of perceptions, thoughts and feelings, without becoming attached to any one of them – attending to the stream but not grasping at the fishes in it. This is reminiscent of the methods of ancient Greek sceptics who argued that we should not become entangled in the divisive web of language which tends to pin down or define what is intangible and indefinable. The sceptics thought that as nothing could be said to have a fixed, independent or absolute existence, including human ideas and opinions, it was best to suspend judgement and belief, and not to become attached to either side of an argument. Similarly we could describe *zazen* as sitting in non-attached attention, being aware of the endless creative play of opposites and possibilities, without taking sides.

*

Creativity is a process, a being-at-home with what occurs from moment to moment, being alive to the potential out of which all events and forms arise – a playfulness in the way we engage with ideas and life. It is also a state of not grasping at what passes, not standing in the way of, or trying to hang on to, the flux of life – creativity is both 'skilful means' and awakening to the way things are.

124   Interwoven Nature

We are surrounded by examples of human creativity in daily life. From the endless creativity of gardeners and householders who raise crops, transform their urban patch of ground, customise doors and house-fronts, to the high-quality graffiti produced by individuals, often with no visual training. Skateboarding is sometimes done with exuberance, skill and high levels of inventiveness. At village fairs homemade cakes are made and decorated with artistry. Every day we pass in the street people who dress in creative ways, lending surprise and beauty to the morning walk to work. We pass enigmatic and thought-provoking signs and phrases that give us pause for thought and laughter. Street entertainers offer us wonderful manifestations of creative movement, music, magic and living-sculpture stillness. A garden shed is lavished with so much raw untutored artistry that we have to return for a second and third look. Because we are surrounded by the vernacular arts and by domestic inventiveness we can easily forget to recognise how creative people are in their homes and workplaces. Without any formal training many, if not most, people have a gift for some kind of creative practice: verbal, manual, technical or social. While some people exercise their creativity in provocative and possibly 'anti-social' ways, others use endlessly inventive ways of de-fusing tension, bringing people together or bringing about social, cultural or political change.

*

The composer, artist and influential thinker, John Cage, recounted how, when he was young, he wanted to change the world. When he realised he wouldn't be able to do this, he became somewhat frustrated and despondent, until he realised that although he couldn't change the world he could change the way he viewed the world - he could change himself and how he thought and acted. This insight led first to greater harmony and a sense of well-being, and also to a life of endless creativity in which in a curious way he did 'change the world' – or at least that part of the world we call music and art.

Cage spent his career encouraging us to open our ears to the soundworld that surrounds us all the time, and to open our minds to indeterminacy, to chance events and the endless surprising routine of everyday life, which, once we get our preconceptions and thinking habits out of the way, can be a source of endless delight and wonder. For Cage this is the way to live a creative life.

Here are some fragments of Cage's writings re-orchestrated by me to give a flavour of his thought:

> *Our poetry now is the realisation that we possess nothing*
> *Out of a hat comes revelation & a pianist. On the way, she said she would play slowly. On the way she would play slowly. She said on the way she would play, play slowly. Everything, he said, is repetition. Slowly she would play. She would say playing slowly she hoped to avoid making mistakes, but there are no mistakes – only sounds, intended & unintended. A glass of brandy*
> *There are already so many sounds to listen to. Why then do we need to make music?*
> *We must work at looking with no judgement, nothing to say. All art has the signature of anonymity*
> *Art is a job that will keep us in a state of not knowing the answers*

*

The Scottish poet Kathleen Jamie suggests that poets are listeners, carefully attending to the goings-on in the world, including the world of the mind:

> When we were young, we were told that poetry is about voice […] but the older I get I think […] it's about listening and the art of listening, listening with attention. I don't just mean with the ear; bringing the quality of attention to the world. The writers I like best are those who attend.[14]

Jamie connects the act of attending, of listening, to the act of praying. When her husband was seriously ill with pneumonia, a friend asked if she had prayed, to which she replied that she hadn't in any formal sense. But, she went on,

> I had noticed […] the cobwebs and the shoaling light and the way the doctor listened and the flecked tweed of her skirt… Isn't that a kind of prayer? The care and maintenance of the web of our noticing, the paying heed?[15]

*

Although poets and artists are seen by many as having special gifts or insights, much of the time it is only that they attend to what is around them in a non-discriminatory way, they are *mindful*. It is in *how* and *what* they notice, and how they share their perceptions with others, that their creativity is demonstrated. They often notice and value what is unnoticed and unvalued by others. In this way the ordinary becomes extraordinary and the mundane takes on a vivid hue.

Sometimes it's enough to see something on the way to work:

> on the road to
> the station a one-eyed
> seagull meets a
> man with a large
> head

Or to notice the whole of a season embodied in one small incident:

> summer on the blue rocks
> a fly scratches

To put everything I've said about creativity in another form:

> Fresh turn again to ideas familiar strange. Immeasurable
> dance of action being chance surprise. Standing thinking,
> every human chaos. Sewing shut to open smooth round
> stone. Illogical leap to incomplete, as small disturbed bird
> on twig in dappled mind all stippled calls to trout. Whatever
> turns to bulls-eye works. So to make a mess, try this, try that,
> give up, go home. Turn again to dance with chance unfolding
> rhetoric of surprise. Full circle to chase wild goose. Lucid
> elusive river-run. Awakening to each fish that flicks its tail,
> one fish after another after another - sudden light
> hitting dappled dark, river-stones turned to silver eels

or, in **Issa**'s (1763-1827) words:

> simply trust
> do not the petals flutter down,
> just like that[16]

---

[1] From the poem, *Pied Beauty*, in Hopkins 1963: 30
[2] Vasari 1965: 325
[3] Haskel 1989: xxx
[4] Weschler 1982
[5] Uchiyama 1990: 52
[6] *ibid*
[7] Dreyfus 2003
[8] Uchiyama 1990: 54
[9] see Watts 1989: 96-97
[10] see Harmless 2007: 208
[11] Harada 1998: 60
[12] *ibid*: 164
[13] see Kim 2010
[14] in Scott 2005: 23
[15] *ibid*
[16] in Blyth 1949: 207

128 Interwoven Nature

XI. THE OLD MAN HAS DREAMS AND NIGHTMARES

Sometimes I catch the scent of the future: a promised land or a hell-on-earth. Sometimes I can't tell which is which.

I see before me a parched land, strewn with empty buildings. At the sea's edge a few shelters have been built with timbers from old houses, lumps of concrete dragged to form walls, tattered plastic sheeting making a flimsy roof. On a hillside I see terraces no longer sharp-edged and clean. The walls have collapsed in many places and brambles climb over fences, gates have fallen. On the south-facing slopes a few bushes cling to the barren soil, deep fissures cut through the contours as if giant teeth have bitten the land trying to find nourishment. On a few north-facing slopes trees grow thinly, live ones interspersed with pale fingers of dead oaks and ash. The landscape looks distraught, perplexed at the neglect shown to it after centuries and ages of care. The sun burns the earth with a kind of fevered hatred. A thin stream trickles along the centre of a wide river-bed, seemingly lost in the shadow of its ancient predecessor. Overhead a few buzzards circle slowly in the rising heat. On a tree-stump a raven sits preening. But no birds sing. Insects buzz and hum. Flies and gnats swirl in complicated patterns over the ribbon of water. But no melody of robin or blackbird leavens the heavy air, no song of territorial claim or amorous exuberance enlivens the sun-baked gloom.

What happened to the plenitude of beings, the overflowing extravagance of creatures and plants, and trees so heavy with blossom and seeds? Where have the small birds gone – the tireless musicians who lightened the day with melodic art? Many years ago, from their spinning seeds ash trees grew in abundance, an annual tide of seedlings that needed the hard work of gardeners to keep them from overwhelming a flower bed. Now, the days are rare when I find one, and to sing of the ash grove is to sing of days long gone, for there are none. Elms are stunted, oaks seem misshapen and unhealthy, pines hardly reach the height of a man before succumbing to one disease or another. I rarely find a frog much less a toad. House sparrows have become exotic beings, chirping and chattering in a quaint dialect I hardly ever hear. Long summer rains are succeeded by parched hot spells when leaves begin to shrivel and cracks appear in the stone-hard soil. Winters are mild then harsh, short then long. Floods happen often in unlikely places. Villages by the sea are abandoned, left to the hungry waves.... I see all of this in my mind and read of the beginnings of it in the few newspapers that come my way. Is this how it will be when I'm gone? Is this what we have left to those who are newly born?

But all things pass and it has always been so. And we will go. Words come back to me, of a voyager, a boatsman - full of the wisdom that travel can bring and the sadness that is woven into every life:

> *Eras flicker away*
> *the gaudy glories of empires fade*
> *gold-sowing kings take their bow*
> *glittering warriors, who killed dragons*
> *and trolls, turn to dust*
>
> *wrinkled lords lean on sticks*
> *as does every man, regardless*
> *of power or wealth*
>
> *old age sits on every shoulder*
> *tongues can no longer taste*
> *sweetness of mead, eyes can*
> *no longer weep, arms cannot*
> *raise a spear or guide a plough*
> *minds no longer think fast or*
> *clever*
>   *each life fades away,*
> *even as it*
> *begins*[1]

Standing by the sea, many years ago, I watched the tide coming in in its usual indiscernible, remorseless way. Inch by inch the wavelets darkened the sand, slipping back only to come forward a little more. The horizon was almost not there — the faintest of tonal change from sea to sky. A fine rain hung in the air beneath seal-grey clouds. Sometimes a moment of quiet noticing reveals the unexpected — a fathoming of quickening truth:

> cormorant
> at high tide
> stands on a post
> black against
> silver rain
>
> dark scripture
> of wings tells all
> and nothing about
> past and future
>
> but it seems
> today there is
> nothing more
> eloquent

Sometimes on mild evenings I used to stand on the ivy-clad balcony looking out over the city and recite aloud a litany of animals that needed special protection because of their uncertain hold on the ladder of survival. My voice merged into an evensong of birds and insects that filled the air around the house. It was my prayer, an oration as poetic as it was scientific — full of rhymes, hypnotic rhythms and resonant naming of species.

132   Interwoven Nature

Mammals: water vole, dolphins, whales, wildcat, otter, pine marten, dormouse, walrus, red squirrel, bats. Reptiles: slow worm, loggerhead sea turtle, green sea turtle, smooth snake, leatherhead sea turtle, hawksbill turtle, sand lizard, viviparous lizard, Kemp's Ridley sea turtle, grass snake, adder.
Amphibians: common toad, natterjack toad, common frog, great crested newt, palmate newt, smooth newt. Fish: sturgeon, Allis shad, Twaite shad, basking shark, vendace, whitefish, giant goby, Couch's goby, turbot, short-snouted seahorse, spiny seahorse, angel shark.

Butterflies: purple emperor, high brown fritillary, northern brown argus, pearl-bordered fritillary, checkered skipper, large heath, small blue, mountain ringlet, marsh fritillary, Duke of Burgundy, silver-spotted, wood white, large copper, adonis blue, chalkhill blue, large blue, Glanville fritillary, heath fritillary, large tortoiseshell, swallowtail, silver-studded blue, black hairstreak, white-letter hairstreak, brown hairstreak, Lulworth skipper.

Moths: reddish buff, fiery clearwing, Fisher's estuarine moth, barberry carpet, black-veined, Sussex emerald, Essex emerald, New Forest burnet. Beetles: rainbow leaf beetle, mire pill beetle, water beetle, lesser silver water beetle, violet click beetle, stag beetle.

Hemipteran bugs: New Forest cicada. Crickets: wart-biter, mole cricket, field cricket.

Dragonflies: Norfolk aeshna, southern damselfly. Spiders: fen raft spider, ladybird spider.

Crustaceans: Atlantic stream crayfish, fairy shrimp, lagoon sand shrimp, apus . Sea-mats: trembling sea-mat. Molluscs: fan mussel, De Folin's lagoon snail, sandbowl snail, Roman snail, pearl mussel, Carthusian snail, glutinous snail, lagoon snail, lagoon sea slug, northern hatchet-shell. Annelid worms: tentacled lagoon-worm, lagoon sandworm, medicinal leech. Sea anemones and allies: marine hydroid, Ivell's sea anemone, pink sea-fan, starlet sea anemone.

Some names I'd say again and again, savouring the words: dormouse, walrus, dormouse, walrus; short-snouted seahorse, short-snouted seahorse. 'Fiery clearwing' would always be followed by a pause as I tried to imagine a wing that was both clear and fiery. For some reason I always whispered 'Norfolk aeshna' – 'aeshna' left hanging in the air like a long sigh. And I could never say 'trembling sea-mat' without smiling and frowning at the same time - because I never knew what a sea-mat was and why this one trembled? Why did the sea anemones need allies any more than the poor solitary New Forest cicada? 'Starlet sea anemone' was a poignant ending to the roll-call – as I imagined a young swaying many-armed diva with pink skin and red lips, soon to be cast away by a stern cold-hearted film producer on the look-out for a new tasty young thing.

After this incantation I would try to bring to mind the birds that were too numerous to name, and all the plants and other organisms that decorated the earth with such splendour and were now besieged on all sides by climatic calamities and human wants and thoughtlessness. I wondered how much time I had and how long it would take to list them all? How much time have they got to be named and honoured, and how long to be forgotten? These questions were usually swallowed by the gathering darkness as I sat quietly watching the twinkling lights of a city that seemed never to hear my prayer that was more like a requiem.

---

[1] The old man may be misremembering an extract from The Seafarer, another text in The Exeter Book – it most closely resembles the translation by Robert Briscoe.

134 Interwoven Nature

XII. BEING HERE – THIS WORLD *IS* HEAVEN

> 'Where does all this throng and stack
> of being, so rich, so distinctive [...]
> come from / nothing I see can answer me'.
> Gerard Manley Hopkins.[1]

We inhabit this planet, not another, and though we trawl the heavens for signs of other planets upon which life might exist we have no way of getting to such a place even if we were successful in our search. This benevolent earth is the source of life and the compass of our being. There is no alternative place to which we might move. So let us make the most out of being here and be creative in our engagement with the world – recognising that the earth is a place of unending mystery, open to infinite avenues of enquiry and celebration. Let us be thankful for being here and let us ensure the well-being of our fellow living organisms – for it is they that help ensure our own survival.

Though our planet provides the optimum conditions for sustaining life, marking it out as very special, if not unique in the known universe, we are causing grave damage to the earth's ecology. This damage affects both the short and long-term capacity of the planet to sustain life. The current crisis in the capitalist system, a crisis often described as financial, economic or the product of faulty banking, is symptomatic of deep-rooted western attitudes to the world in which we live. These attitudes are essentially exploitative, based on a fallacious idea that the earth's resources are infinite and are thus able to support limitless numbers of human beings, each seeking to satisfy his or her individual needs, desires and aspirations. Once individuals within a society, or, usually, an elite within that society, have gained the capacity to live comfortably, relatively secure in the knowledge that they have food, shelter and a reasonable life-expectancy, they then begin to want more and more: more money, more material goods, a rise in status and the satisfaction of other desires which always seem to exceed the possibility of fulfilment. The comfortable elite, in societies all around the globe, are continually adding to a wish-list of supplementary wants that rapidly become essential needs. This desire for more, better, greater and bigger is what fuels the consumer engine that drives the capitalist machine. The satisfaction of this desire is, almost by definition, unachievable (because there is no end to the wish-list) and, given the finite resources of the earth, unsustainable.

Add to this the fact that a huge number of human beings, living at best in discomfort, at worst in debilitating states of poverty, malnutrition and disease, are desperate to satisfy their genuine needs for food, shelter and the means for an adequate livelihood – then the demands on the world's resources become even more unsustainable. This is not because of the latter group's reasonable desire for a very basic standard of living, but because of the unreasonable desire of the comfortable elite to have more, better and bigger – for it is the satisfaction of these supplementary wants that is unsustainable. Indeed, it may be that the consumer demands of the comfortable elite militate against the countless millions of poor and hungry ever being able to satisfy even their most basic needs.

Somehow we have to develop more sustainable, and more just and equitable, means of production, and we have to recognise the role our own desires and satisfactions play in this kind of transaction. Perhaps even small changes of behaviour on our part, (as most of us are members of the comfortable elite), could improve matters. Becoming more keenly aware of what we need, as opposed to what we desire over and above our needs, might enable us to moderate our desires and to reduce our consumption in ways that will mitigate the worse effects these have on other people and on the planet.

*

In order to understand our true needs and to see more clearly who we are and how we are as beings, we have to be able to observe the workings of our embodied minds in a dispassionate and balanced way. This kind of mindful observation enables us to revise our understanding of ourselves and to re-fashion our sense of self in a way that aligns more closely with our actual experience and with how we are in the world. It is this revisioning of ourselves in the world that I would now like to discuss.

We live in a relational universe, a universe of interwoven and interactive processes and energies – a universe in which *things* are actually *events*, with no fixed essences or identities. All is in flux, merging and mingling in changing patterns of dynamic kinship. We are relational beings.

According to the Chinese poet, Han Shan (who lived sometime in the 7th or 8th Century):

> The peach blossoms would like to stay
>   through the summer
> But the winds and moons hurry them on and
>   will not wait[2]

Given that everything is subject to change, all entities can only ever be provisional and contingent, subject to processes of restructuring, decay and dissolution, however fast or slow. Every entity will become something else and has been something else. Mutation and transformation are the norm, not the exception. In this sense we inhabit a changeful universe, ambiguous, paradoxical and uncertain. We can never be sure where one thing ends and another begins, including where we end and someone else begins. The self is not a hermetically sealed kernel or soul, absolute and unchanging, it is a dynamic interweaving of streams of being – of perceptions, emotions, thoughts, imaginative constructions, memories and aspirations – a network of relationships with no fixed perimeter. Our boundaries are fluid, indeterminate and inextricably interwoven into the shifting boundaries of everything else in the universe. Our corporeal skin is a semi-permeable membrane through which moisture, light, tiny organisms and sub-atomic particles pass. Likewise our minds are permeable indefinite structures flowing with experiences, of every imaginable kind. Our very being is fluid and many-stranded, and not contained within definite mental, physical, social or cultural boundaries.

As we have seen, the German philosopher, Martin Heidegger, provides a useful way of thinking about the self and the nature of our being-in-the-world. Heidegger conceives of being as a field of care and concern that is not co-extensive with a particular human body, but is rather an open network of fluid relationships with others and with the world. Heidegger calls this field of being, *Dasein* – which can be translated from the German as 'being-there'. In Heidegger's view *Dasein* is without essence, it is indeterminate, a field of possibilities, some of which can be actualised by an individual in the course of his or her life. And each person's field 'of care and concern' is a social space, overlapping, merging and interacting with the fields of other beings. The self is the agent of care and concern and the channel through which care flows in, out and through us. Dasein, 'being-there', is also 'being-with' or 'being-together' – it is a reciprocal and ever-changing state of relationship with others and with the world. We exist in a state of interdependence with everything that exists.

Buddhists describe this state of interbeing, interpenetration and interdependence as 'dependent co-arising' or 'dependent origination', awkward phrases that are translations of the Sanskrit term, *pratītyasamutpāda* – which combines the word, *pratītya*, meaning 'meeting, relying, depending', with the word, *samutpa*, meaning 'arising'.

From the Buddhist perspective there are no separate entities – all phenomena arise within a relational field, bound together by causal relationships extending through space and time. Everything is co-dependent on everything else and everything is in a state of change. There are no fixed essences or identities – for change and interdependence penetrate every entity.

This is equally true for us human beings. None of us can be considered as separate, existing for, or of, ourselves. We are deeply porous beings, overlapping, merging and interweaving with our surroundings and with other beings, including our human co-habitants of planet earth. Just as our bodies are porous, our minds aren't bounded by our bodies or by our conventional sense of self. Our being is both a function of our body's negotiation of our surroundings, firmly located in this space we occupy, *and* a non-localised web of connections and dependencies with those for whom we care, and who care for us, with the other organisms who share our envelope of skin, and with all the tissues of ideas, stories, beliefs and values that constitute our cultural commons.

the relational field of our care and concern ... interbeing

The term, *pratītyasamutpāda*, dependent origination, also alludes to the currents of causality that are interwoven through the universe, and through us – the causal relationships that give rise to things as they are, to us as we are. One thing leads to another, one action or event gives rise to another, and another – causal effects that ripple out in every direction. If we consider plastic as an example, we notice that plastic comes from oil; oil from fossils; fossils from ancient life forms; these life forms evolved over millennia from other life forms going back to single-cell organisms; and prior to that to chemical interactions, and to the 'big bang' origin of the universe; and maybe to other 'big bangs' and other universes. This great web of interdependence gives rise to plastic, indeed plastic could be said to be a manifestation of this stream of cause and effect – a piece of plastic, in some way, contains or includes, all these other phenomena. Likewise, this chair that I sit on is its own history, bound up in its present. It is the coming together of all the forces, actions, ideas and materials that went into its making, and that went into their making, and so on, and so on, throughout time and space. The chair exists in the way that it does, because everything else in the universe exists as it does. Things are as they are, because other things are as they are, because everything is as it is. Change one thing and all things change.

> Each can only be what it is
> yet it depends on all it is not
> - for the stone is only what
> the universe displays to itself
> when every fibre is aligned
> just so, move the most distant
> thing and the stone will not be
> what it seems to be
>
> the stone is the stone and
> all that is not the stone

Causal relationships and dependent origination extend to all phenomena, a continually changing web of mutual influences and connections. Not only are past and future implicated in each other, but they are also contained in the present. This interdependence is an endless process. Nothing is ever fixed as it is, because everything is always subject to change, growth, decay, revision and transformation – the universe is provisional, contingent, conditional.

As Thich Nhat Hanh puts it: 'This is, because that is. This is not, because that is not. This ceases to be, because that ceases to be.'[3]

I've tried to express this in a poem entitled, Nothing is what it is:

> like mercury,
> but dancing,
> river-sea surface,
> tide-high, reaches
> at rocks, catches
> at a low wet
> sky
>
> mist salves the wounds
> of autumned oaks
> turning yellow on fading
> hills
>
> objects are widowed of shape
> and essence, nothing is what
> it is without its
> absence
>
> empty mist,
> up close,
> is a plenitude
> of drops, an ocean
> of reflected
> worlds

*

We can approach the concept of interdependence from another perspective and think about the making of boundaries and divisions. In his book, No Boundary, Ken Wilbur talks about the human practice of naming and labelling: 'in the book of Genesis, one of the first tasks given to Adam is to name the animals and plants existing in nature. For nature doesn't come ready-labelled with name tags…'[4] Labelling is an extension of the process of categorising, dividing and sorting – all of which depend on boundary defining – drawing boundaries around things. A boundary always marks off one thing from another: an inside from an outside, this from that, sea from sky, me from you. The inside and outside don't exist until the boundary is drawn. And yet a boundary belongs as much to the inside as to the outside, the boundary joins as much as it separates. In this way, as pointed out by Nicolas of Cusa, inside and outside can't be separated, they arise together and are interdependent – a 'coincidence of opposites.'

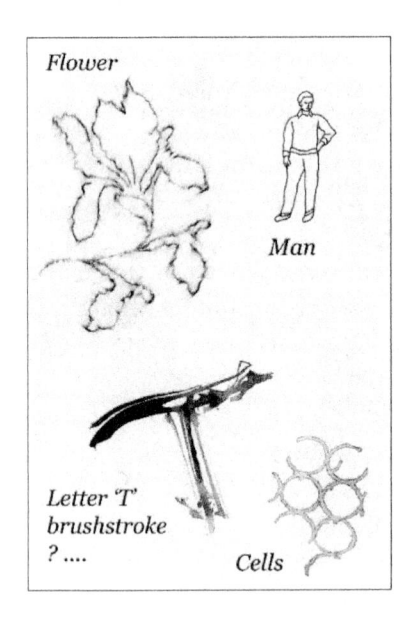

Flower

Man

Letter 'T' brushstroke ? ....

Cells

In Hindu and Buddhist terminology the world of boundaries, categories, labels and all dualities is known as *maya* – that is *nama* and *rupa*, name and form – the naming of forms. By drawing a boundary we define a form and isolate an object out of the indefinite and ineffable flux of the universe – a process of constant evolution and change is replaced by a thing, an object, a human construct. We then begin to believe in a world of defined objects and nouns, rather than a reality of processes and verbs. The boundaries are drawn by humans, maintained by convention and reinforced by belief and habit. In reality, in nature, there are no separating boundaries and no dualities engendered by boundaries.

It is easy to see how we can become so used to deploying boundaries, names and labels that we begin to forget that they are human constructions maintained by convention – instead, we start to believe in them as facts that constitute reality. To believe in the label as a condition or essence of reality is to be deluded – just as we are deluded if we believe that the two-dimensional face in the mirror *is* the three-dimensional face looking at the mirror. And yet we have a tendency to live our lives believing that boundaries and labels, and the objectified forms they define, are fundamental attributes of reality, and we lose sight of the boundary-less, interwoven and changeful nature of existence-as-it-is.

Ken Wilbur quotes from the Bhagavad Gita: 'For he that is freed from pairs [duality, divisions, boundaries] is easily freed from conflicts.'[5] For boundaries delineate two entities where once there was one and, so often, the two become polarities in an arena in which contrasting choices, judgments and beliefs are contested. We cling to our judgments and beliefs as if they are vital to our existence and disputes arise as we argue our position with ever-greater vehemence. The boundless becomes the bounded and the bounded are set against each other – oppositions arise and conflict ensues. We see how this happens in all spheres of human activity: from arguments over this or that piece of bounded territory, to this or that opinion, idea or belief.

Wilbur reminds us that this chain of causality from unbounded interwoven reality to clearly defined separate objects needs to be broken, or at least recognised and taken account of. We need to be aware of the process of drawing boundaries, to see the process for what it is, and to observe how it affects how we experience and think about ourselves. Wilbur writes:

> My mind, my body, my thoughts, my desires – these are no more my real Self than the trees, the stars, the clouds, and the mountains, for I can witness *all* of them as objects, with equal felicity. Proceeding in this fashion, I become transparent to my Self, and realise that in some sense what I am goes much,

much beyond this isolated, skin-bound organism. The more I go into I, the more I fall out of I.⁶

Like many mystics (Christian, Moslem and Buddhist) Wilbur argues that there is no clear, and certainly no fixed boundary, separating the self from the universe. The self is in many ways unbounded and inseparable from the universe. We could even say, as many have done, that the self *is one* with the universe. Any apparent boundary is at the very least artificial and conventional – a flimsy marker that has no substantial reality.

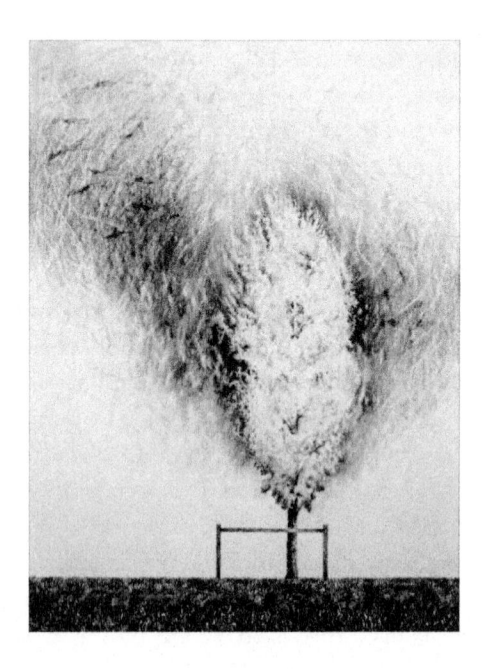

'Tree' is a word we use as shorthand for referring to a complex array of substances, forms, chemical and biological processes, relationships, narratives and associations. The living tree is very different to a dead tree in that it grows, extends its branches, flowers, bares seed and moves in the breeze, but even a dead tree contains life – the lives of innumerable organisms that inhabit, digest, make use of and transform the substance of the tree. In this sense the difference between living and dead is one of degree rather than absolute distinction. The life of the tree continues into its dying and decay.

We can think of the tree as a society, a community of organisms, co-habiting the same space, sharing air, soil, sunlight and rain, within a larger community of hedgerow, copse, wood and forest, or huddled against a granite tor on some inhospitable moor or mountainside. The actual tree, whether dead or alive, to which we point with the word *tree*, is less an object and more an organic event or conglomeration of biological processes.

Similarly when we refer to a person, a particular human being, we refer to a complex array of features and processes: an organism; an embodied mind woven into a culture – a web of social and familial relationships; a tangle of actions, hopes, aspirations, feelings, thoughts, memories and stories; acts of kindness and meanness, selflessness and selfishness, likes and dislikes, friendships and enmities; with ties to dogs, cats, birds, places, ideas and beliefs.

A person is also a history of encounters, experiences, cares and tribulations, joys and sorrows. It is this stream of qualities and characteristics that constitutes the person who stands before us, or who we remember. And, as we have seen, the person is not a skin-bounded presence, separate from the rest of the universe, but a congregation of organisms, bacteria, cells and atoms, pulsing together in dynamic and harmonious interdependence. Human beings are inscribed and interwoven with each other and with other beings and with the great web of impermanence we call the universe.

It is worth quoting at length a beautiful evocation, by Tim Flannery, of what constitutes a human being:

> And there is me. Billions of cells cooperating seamlessly at every moment and a brain made up of a reptilian stem, a middle mammalian portion, and two highly evolved yet relatively poorly connected hemispheres somehow add up to that thing I call me. And beyond that miracle of cooperation

is my wider world, made up of a web of loves that I could not live without: spouse, children, parents, friends [...] Beyond my family circle there is my city with its millions of residents, my country, which coordinates actions through a ballot box, and beyond that my planet with its countless dependent parts. Our world is a web of interdependencies woven so tightly that it sometimes becomes love.[7]

*

I also remember a passage in David Stacton's novel, Segaki: 'though nature is unmoved by even the finest of our desires, it is always waiting to get its chemicals back again, for it can only survive by the constant redistribution of its constituent parts, which it lends to one thing or another, here a crystal of feldspar, there a peninsula or a man.'[8] The atoms that make up my body are on loan from the great atomic storehouse out of which all things are loaned and made. This is kinship and interdependence expressed in a different way.

*

When we walk amongst trees we feel the air around us, washing over our faces and hands. We perceive the air, the trees, birds, mosses, earth and glimpses of sky. We *are* these experiences. We *are* the sounds, the scent and taste of the moving air. We are what we are because of those who came before – a stream of evolution going back to the first organisms almost four billions years ago. As we stop and stand close to this tree – it's a giant sequoia in a Devon park – we breathe as the tree breathes. We breathe out carbon dioxide. The chlorophyll in each tiny flat leaf or needle absorbs carbon dioxide, mixes it with water drawn up by the tree roots and breathes out oxygen and water vapour. We breathe in the oxygen. In this way we and the tree breathe as one. We are interdependent strands of one great cycle of respiration and life.

A giant sequoia like this, growing in northern California, can stand over three-hundred feet tall and live for up to three thousand years. It is one of the largest organisms ever to grace the earth. The snowdrops growing near the base of this Devon sequoia are small and their flowers only bloom for a couple of weeks. Each has its own rhythm and time. Both will pass, as does a cloud or a mountain.

A famous Zen poem goes like this:

> the morning-glory
> that lives but for a day
> differs not at heart
> from the giant pine
> that lives for a thousand years.

Each breath is like a life – with each inbreath and outbreath we live and die. With each step we take we can be at home in the here and now, at home in our porous breathing bodies – at one with the snowdrop and the tree, with all beings and with the world.

*

We are not bound by our body, but freed by it – opened by its pores and openings to the light and shade, the weightless substance, of the world. The body is our liminal domain, not our binding perimeter. The skin is as much of the world and of others, as it is of my-self. And the embodied mind is always in motion, flowing through and dancing around the skin and bones – a gathering and intermingling of trajectories that are as much 'yours' as they are 'mine', as much the product of interaction and interpenetration with the world (and with others) as they are generated by the ego-self. Ideas arise in the space between, the flow around, a community of human beings, and in the conversations and debates that are integral to our human imagination and action.

> so many openings
> through which the world
> enters,
>   mingles,
> melts into me
>
>   only to flow on
> into others, world

into self, self into
world,

like sticks in a stream,
bent by the light, we
pass through a prism

rainbowed and scattered

we are not what we
seem

When I observe my own consciousness I perceive currents of identity, strands of personality, constantly forming and re-forming, weaving complex patterns – intricately interwoven with the lives of other beings (human and non-human). I don't observe a solitary nucleus of self, separate and unchanging.

Looking inwards is also looking outwards; to observe my being is to observe all beings; to observe myself is to observe the world.

We're not defined by any particular current of our being – our gender, our pain, our physical make-up, our hopes, our fears, our illness, our roles, our talents, our strengths or our weaknesses – these are all interwoven strands that combine in the fluid stream of experience that we refer to as 'me' or 'myself'. The many currents of our being are engaged in a process of forming and reforming that is without end.

When we observe the many currents of being, we notice that the changing forms they give rise to – 'me' or 'you' or that bird or insect over there – are always indefinable and indefinite, yet distinctive and marvellously varied.

[1] Hopkins 1963: 145
[2] Watson 1970: 16
[3] Hanh 1999: 221-222
[4] Wilbur 1981: 17
[5] ibid: 27
[6] ibid: 57
[7] Flannery 2011: 30-31
[8] Stacton 2012: 55

150   Interwoven Nature

XIII. THE OLD MAN SITS ON THE BALCONY

For many days now, after short nights of fitful sleep, I come out onto the balcony and sit quietly watching, noticing, feeling. Thoughts come and go. I see them clearly, like bubbles of words rising in a glass of water. Each one expands until it bursts, dissolving back into the transparent space. Somehow, they no longer have a hold on me, they no longer drag me from place to place. I watch them and smile. How can it be that I once thought life's puzzles and pains might be solved by the next thought? How strange it now seems that every new idea brought excitement and hope, often followed by faint disappointment and a hollowness that waited to be filled again.

I watch clouds of feeling and memory passing through my mind. They seem to have no substance. No weight. They're no longer attached to me, as clouds aren't tethered to the sky. Squalls of anxiety blow through, whipping up waves as they go. But the waves are small and short-lived. There's a steadiness and balance to my days, that no squall or thunder can disturb.

As I gaze out over the city I hear the mad rush of traffic, footsteps, voices, sirens…. everyone scurrying here and there, driven by deadlines and ambitions and the frantic desire for things…. so much wanting for what will never be enough… so much fruitless labour and dreaming about tomorrow or yesterday. My heart goes out to them. Their folly is my folly. For most of my life I've scurried from dream to dream, desire to desire, hope to hope. As if what I did next would somehow bring satisfaction and peace. But, of course, it didn't. It only brought a familiar feeling of despondency and the kindling of another round of fruitless seeking. It was as if I was so intent on what lay around the next corner that I couldn't see what was right in front of me. So much running and stumbling, climbing and falling, clutching at phantoms that dissolved as I touched them.

Maybe it has always been so, this compelling carousel that holds us in its thrall, leaving us breathless, dizzy, yet anxious for another go. For it is a fairground. We are children with candyfloss and toffee apples in our hands. We run from ride to ride, full of energy and expectancy. Even as we feel nauseous we climb on to another whirligig machine that spins us ever on.

> *myself I see*
> *in the urgent wanderings*
> *of the fly*

Yet now, in my elder days, I no longer feel the need to climb on the carousel, maybe my knees are too painful, or I've grown tired of the spinning ways. Now I sit and watch, noticing what I'd not seen before, realising how futile it is to get on a spinning machine in the hope that it will take me anywhere other than back to where I started.

These thoughts take me back to my boyhood, to my teenage years when I dreamt of becoming a Zen monk. I pledged that I'd would work hard at my meditation, serve the abbot as best I could, study the writings of all the Zen masters and strive for enlightenment like my Zen master heroes Dogen, Bankei and homeless Kodo. I sat in my bedroom in the big granite house my parents had bought some years before. I read through the meagre supply of books on Buddhism in my local library and began to sit in meditation following the instructions given by master Dogen in the thirteenth century: sit in a quiet place …set aside all opinions and attachments …don't be concerned with notions of good and bad … set aside your desire to become enlightened …just sit at peace and be at one with the universe …observe whatever arises in your mind with equanimity …sit up straight, alert yet relaxed …breath gently through the nose, watching each breath as if it is your last …

Deep down I knew I would never leave my family and travel to Japan but I followed Dogen's advice as best I could. Getting my legs into a lotus position was impossible, but I could kneel with my bottom perched on cushions folded into a firm support. Every evening and at weekends my spare time was devoted to sitting meditation – 'zazen' as Dogen called it. Often I'd sit with my mind racing from thought to thought, image to image, idea to idea. I'd become entangled in contradictory feelings and impulses: how can I not strive to be enlightened when that is what I want most of all? How can I not think of what is good and bad, *when I'm trying to be good and not to be bad? How can I be at peace when I'm besieged by doubts and uncertainties and can't be sure I'm sitting as Dogen tells me to?*

Every time I sat I tried to observe each breath and often felt I could discern no point at which the inbreath became an outbreath, there was no definite gap between one and the other. As my breath steadied and grew ever gentler I could no longer feel the moment when out turned to in. No matter how attentive I was I could observe no boundary between breaths – the turning point had disappeared. It was as if there was only one breath, or one breathing, for it was a fluid process, not a series of separate states. I noticed this was true with all manner of things: feelings, thoughts, images that came to mind – they flowed one into another in a constant stream without definite boundaries or beginnings or endings.

And I came to realise that this was true of all phenomena. If I observed carefully enough I could see fewer and fewer clear edges. Later, when I started to draw from observation in line or tone, even things that seemed clear cut, like a sharp jagged granite rock had a penumbra of uncertainty around it, a hazy hinterland where the rock met the air, the grey met the blue, the dark met the light. Any line I drew was provisional and even as it marked an edge to something it also marked a joining, a connecting, a binding together of one thing to another. Drawing made me realise how arbitrary were the lines we put around things. How lines, edges and distinctions were conventions that were useful in some ways (for talking about

things, describing, analysing, counting) but were not how the world is, for the universe is boundary-less and boundless.

I realised that to sit in zazen is very simple yet extremely difficult. It involves nothing more, or less, than sitting in full attention to the here and now - being-here - observing the mind in tranquillity without commenting or clinging to the experiences, thoughts, feelings and sensations that make up consciousness. When I look back to my childhood I realise that my earliest experience of this kind of mindful, undivided attention was as an animal watcher. In the years before I'd heard of zazen or meditation I spent hours and hours out in the woods and heathland near my home, waiting for birds and animals to arrive at the place I'd chosen to sit – usually a rock, or a small clearing, or the foot of a tree.

I noticed that if I was agitated, or too hopeful, the birds and animals would notice me and keep their distance. But if I gave up any intention of being a bird-watcher, if I let go of my excitement, anticipation and hope, they would often wander right up to me – almost as if I wasn't there. And in a sense, I wasn't there. That is, the egocentric, unitary, 'I', wasn't there. Instead a different state of being was at work (or at play) – as if the edges of myself were dissolved into the surrounding space. It felt as if there was no separation between me and the world. As if the blackbirds, wrens, gorse linnets, and the occasional fox and badger that wandered by, were other essays in being, alternative manifestations of the life that flowed within me. It is this state of being that zazen engenders and when I first practiced sitting meditation it felt very familiar, a return to the state that I'd sometimes experienced as a youngster sitting on a rock watching a goldcrest only a few feet away making its carefully constructed nest.

I remember reading Samuel Johnson: 'Nothing is little to him who feels it with great sensibility.'

> *I sweep the dust*
> *along the floor*
> *but the patch of*
> *sunlight will not*
> *be hurried*

Once I sat on a familiar granite slab in a clearing near our house. Around me a half-circle of hillside lumbered upwards, massive rocks tilting at all angles, interspersed with smaller boulders over which mosses and lichens crept inch by inch, casting a mottled yellow-grey light under the big rowan tree that spread out over the hollow. My granite zazen sitting stone was under this tree and I often came to sit here on spring and summer evenings. I rocked side-to-side, backwards and forwards, as I always did to find a settled posture. Then the work began, the gentle work of observing everything that happened, always tethered to the process of watching and feeling and breathing.

On this occasion I'd been there for a while – how long, I don't know, for time seemed as elastic and indefinite as everything else. The breathing was even and shallow, unforced. The mind was quiet with only a few passing thoughts and images. My eyes were open (as always in zazen) and my vision was at rest on the leaf and grass patch in front of me. My visual attention switched from centre to edge, edge to centre, gently scanning. I became aware of movement at the periphery, a russet and grey motion that shifted left and right, growing slightly larger with each movement. This observation was a flicker amongst a field of other sensations flowing in a stream.

On that particular day I was calm, or it was calm, the day was calm, there was peace. Nothing seemed to drag my attention this way and that, no tumbling of thoughts one over another, just this steady being under the rowan tree. The russet and grey grew larger and I can remember only a gentle hum in the air. It was only after what seemed a long spell of watching that a form took shape very close, and a sound of sniffing and panting – a fox was right in front of me. In the still centre of vision, the vivid face and breath and eyes gazed up into mine and there was a look between us that was just a look, not fearful or disturbed, an untroubled peaceful observation that I remember still as one of the key experiences of my life.

Although this was a particularly memorable event I had many such encounters with birds, badgers, deer and mice, both while practicing zazen and, in my younger days, while out playing in the woods or birdwatching amongst the gorse and bilberry bushes. A few years later, while sitting in a clearing in Epping Forest, I caught the faint sound of scrabbling and noticed at the edge of my vision a small patch of dry ground lifting and gently splitting as the pinkish snout of a mole appeared with its two paws held aloft. It turned its head towards me with a baleful look as if to say, 'here we are, now what do we do', before squirming back down its hole and tunnelling away. None of these quiet meetings would have happened in the usual run of things. It was only because there was no sense of threat or disturbance in my presence, nothing to ruffle the sense of wellbeing of the creatures I met, that we could spend time together. Somehow there was a dissolution of the usual boundaries, a fading away of the separations and antagonisms that usually characterise such encounters.

> *who knows when the night ends*
> *and the day begins?*
> *who knows where I end*
> *and you begin?*

The practice of mindfulness, zazen and other modes of contemplation, manifest a very different mode of being to the acquisitive and boundary-making ways in which we often relate to the world and to other beings. While it is necessary, at times, to analyse, acquire, divide and categorise, these modes of thought and behaviour can get out of hand, leaving us with a deepening sense of separation and disconnection from the world. And it is this artificial sense of not belonging, of the world as external or apart from us, that leads us into dangerous waters – for we lose touch with how things are, we lose touch with a primary condition of being: the condition of inter-relationship and interdependence. Somehow, we have to come back to a recognition of this condition and to re-establish our sense of being interwoven with everything else. Clear-sighted contemplation is one method for doing this, a method that has been tried and tested for millennia. By seeing and experiencing the world as it is, boundary-less and boundless, we establish and nourish a counter-balance to acquisitive and divisive modes of being, enabling us to live in harmony with ourselves, with other beings and with the world.

In my old age I have returned to the wisdom of my youth. It has been a long and winding journey, full of mistaken beliefs and wrong turnings, but these meanderings have deepened my sense of return after being confused and sidetracked by games, short-lived pleasures and long-lived dissatisfaction. I can see how rational analysis and enquiry are important ways of coming to an understanding of ourselves and our place in the world, but I also see how they can lead us astray if we become over-reliant on them. Sceptical enquiry is vital to human understanding and development, but analysis without synthesis often leads to misunderstanding and distortion, and this is why we need to develop modes of synthesis and integration manifested in mindful contemplation and zazen. By doing this we can restore our sense of belonging, of unity, of connectedness and harmony.

I gaze out over the city and hear the sounds of scurrying and rushing as my fellows make their way to work and to play and to make sense of themselves and their place in the world. But just as a boy learnt, many years ago, to stop and sit in quiet contemplation, without comment and judgment, letting go of the mistaken sense of separation between himself and his surroundings, so I hope that these citizens will pause, sit on a bench, set aside their desires and opinions, and observe how things really are.

>   *the city glitters in morning sun*
>   *trees glow and shadows deepen*
>   *everyone is serious and full of*
>   *determination, there is no*
>   *problem that cannot be*
>   *solved, nothing that cannot*
>   *be gained or set aside*
>   *all the pleasures of this*
>   *world are here for the taking*
>   *and yet,*
>   *the quickening world*
>   *hurries on and we cannot keep*
>   *pace, the wayside is littered*
>   *with petals and names*
>   *see them blown here and there*

158 Interwoven Nature

XIV. REVISION AND REORIENTATION – REALISING OUR INTERWOVEN NATURE

So far I have explored aspects of our nature that we have tended to misunderstand, marginalise or even deny as we hold on to a view of ourselves as separate from the world, believing that we are bounded by a distinct and impermeable physical and psychological skin that encloses a fixed essence or identity – a nucleic ego or 'I' that looks out at the world and at other beings as alien territory, ripe for consumption and exploitation. I have suggested that this view is misguided and at odds with how things are, for we live in a universe in which all entities are interwoven and interdependent.

In this chapter I want to briefly explore one further characteristic of existence, 'impermanence', and then go on to suggest particular ways in which we can rediscover or realise our interwoven nature and reorient our lives around this realisation.

Many religions have developed ways of recognising and exploring the interconnectedness of self and universe - Christianity, Islam, Judaism, Hinduism and Daoism all manifest modes of prayer and meditation that break down artificial barriers between self, world and 'God'. Many ancient tribal cultures have similar ideas and practices, and contemporary science, particularly physics and ecology, explore states of interconnection, interdependence and change. I am going to discuss another example, Buddhism, which has also developed a formidable experiential enquiry into the nature of the self and its relationship to a world of transience and interpenetration.

Buddhists consider impermanence to be one of the three marks of existence – the other two being: absence of self-existence; and dissatisfaction or suffering. It is useful to examine the Buddhist viewpoint that impermanence permeates existence, and to understand the implications of this view.

Little is known about the historical Buddha. It is quite likely that he belonged to a tribal group – the Shakya or Sakya, hence one of his names, Shakyamuni ('sage of the Shakya clan') – and he may have been the son of a tribal elder. This was before the time of palaces and cities. He probably lived in a large thatched dwelling in the forest, surrounded by his extended family. However according to popular legend, as a child the Buddha was a pampered prince living in wealth and seclusion on his family estate. His parents seem to have done what parents are advised not to do with their children, which is to spoil them with an inordinate amount of love, comfort and security. He was shielded from anything that might suggest that life was anything other than a long holiday. His every need was satisfied and nothing disturbed the cosseted harmony of his life. It was only as a young man that he ventured out into the world beyond his royal estate. What he encountered there came as a great shock to him and prompted questions that he sought to explore for the rest of his life. This traditional narrative, no doubt developed over hundreds of years, may not tally with the historical evidence but it is a useful lens through which to view some key insights of the Buddha.

Inside the family enclosure, Prince Gautama (the Buddha's family name) had seen nothing of poverty and violence, and his parents had even managed to keep illness and death out of his sight. It was only when he left his home that he came face to face with these disturbing aspects of life and he was no doubt perturbed and perplexed by what he confronted. As he travelled he saw poor and hungry peasants trying to feed themselves and their children. He saw babies born, children growing, men and women getting older and frailer, and he saw the bodies of the dead being burned on pyres surrounded by mourners who howled with grief and loss. Wherever he looked he noticed how things change; how the seasons come and go; how flowers bloom and wither; how trees grow from tiny seeds into forest giants only, one day, to fall down and crumble into dust; he saw small rivulets turning into streams, eventually flowing into big rivers that emptied into the sea; he watched clouds changing shape, dropping rain and snow as they reached high mountains; and he noticed how mountains themselves are eroded by rain and ice, avalanches cascading into rivers only to be washed away.

The young prince realised that nothing is exempt from this process of growth and decay. Everywhere around him he encountered only change and impermanence. There is nothing that keeps its form or structure forever. From the smallest butterfly to the highest mountain, there is nothing that isn't passing away even as it comes into being. In this way he came to view impermanence (*anicca*) as the first mark of existence.

If everything changes in this way, he thought, then nothing can have a stable or enduring identity. The core of the tree is subject to change and decay as much as the outer leaves. Eventually even the heart of a mountain is eaten away by the remorseless action of water, ice and wind. Indeed, he could see that one thing becomes another: chicks become birds; caterpillars become moths; frog-spawn turns into tadpoles and then frogs; apple-blossom will one day become an apple – and it doesn't end there: an apple may be eaten by a monkey; the chewed-up apple is digested and monkey droppings are scattered on the forest floor; the monkey dung is eaten by beetles and other creatures, and breaks down into the humus that provides food for the mighty trees. Again, nothing seems to be exempt from this process of recycling: one thing becoming another, over and over again. Everything seems, over time, to merge with everything else. Great chains of connection and causality are woven through the universe, in such a way that nothing stands alone and separate. Everything is interwoven with everything else. The fact that nothing exists separate from anything else and therefore, that nothing has an enduring essence or self-existence, is the second mark of existence – known as *anatta* in Buddhist terminology.

As the young prince continued on his journey he began to notice something that surprised and puzzled him. He saw how people lived their lives, talking, planning and acting as if things were separate and independent of each other, and he saw how people clung to a desire for permanence and unchanging stability – something his parents had been trying to do during his childhood. It was as if everyone hadn't noticed the changing interdependence of everything that surrounded them – as if they were living in a dream world of stability and permanence, afraid to wake up to the ceaselessly changing nature of the actual universe.

On top of the natural sense of loss at the death of an aged parent he could see that many people also suffer because they believe, or rather hope and pray, that no-one *should* die or that no-one *should* become ill or old. It is as if they set themselves against the two marks of existence, trying to deny or ignore the way things are. This attachment to a false understanding of how the world is, causes people to become dissatisfied and frustrated, only adding to their suffering. Dreaming and hoping for permanence, and clinging desperately to things, ideas and other people as they change and pass away, only makes us more unhappy, restless and uneasy. This state of dissatisfaction, unhappiness and unease is the third mark of existence – *dukkha*.

This last mark of existence, the state of unnecessary suffering and dis-ease, is caused by a failure to recognise and live with the inevitability of the other two conditions of life. While the first two marks can't be changed, the third can: by changing the way in which we think about, relate to and experience the world. The young Buddha vowed to devote himself to finding a way to transform his approach to life and to enable everyone to wake up to the first two marks of existence and to alleviate dissatisfaction and unnecessary suffering. His methods for doing this have been tried and tested over centuries and form the basis of contemporary Buddhist practice throughout the world.

One important method for recognising and realising how impermanence and interdependence are primary conditions of existence is mindful meditation, of which there are many variants with different names but sharing common characteristics. Zazen and vipassana are two forms of mindful meditation developed by Japanese Zen Buddhists and by the forest monks and nuns of

Southeast Asia (Theravada Buddhists). Although there are many differences of emphasis in theory and practice, these two approaches can be discussed together as they both consider mindfulness as the key to realisation and are central to what we know of the Buddha's teachings

The essential elements of the Buddha's teachings on mindfulness are presented in the *Satipatthana Sutta* – one of the earliest texts of the Pali Canon, a collection of discourses about the Buddha's life and teachings preserved in oral form until it was written down around the time of the Fourth Buddhist Council in Sri Lanka, c.29 BCE. In this text the Buddha advises his students that the only way to overcome suffering and to develop peace of mind is to pay attention to the stream of experiences that arise in our embodied mind – to observe, as clearly as possible, the flow of sensations, thoughts, emotions and other phenomena that make up our consciousness. Doing this, without attachment or making judgments, or adding our opinions and comments to what we observe, enables us to gain insight into who we are and to realise how interconnected we are with all beings and things. In this way we come to an understanding of the transient nature of existence and develop compassion for ourselves and for others. We feel kinship with all beings and realise that we depend upon each other. This is, according to the Buddha, 'the right path', the Middle Way.

The method of mindful meditation advocated by the Buddha is very similar to zazen (sitting meditation) and vipassana (insight meditation) as they are practiced today in Japan, southeast Asia and in the West. One important aspect of both zazen and vipassana is the use of the breath as a focus of attention. The process of breathing becomes a gateway to a realisation of our interdependence with the world about us, the constant interaction between our embodied mind and the air we breathe. We observe the in-breath and the out-breath as the rhythmic manifestation of the rise and fall of consciousness, the motion of life as we observe it from moment-to-moment. The breath is not forced in any way, we are not trying to make it deeper or shallower - we simply observe it as it is. This steady, patient observation of the breath becomes a gentle discipline of the mind, a way of becoming calm and collected, and it affords us a refuge from whatever turbulence might otherwise be troubling us. Paying attention to the whole sphere of sensations, thoughts, moods and emotions follows on from the practice of being mindful of the breath.

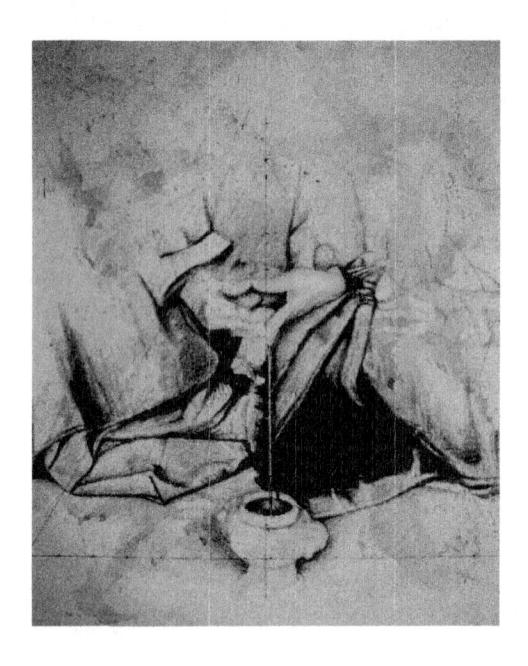

Mindful meditation enables us to experience the self as a process that extends out into the world, we realise how open and porous we are and how interconnected we are with other beings and with our surroundings. We feel less divided from the world about us and less alienated from ourselves and other creatures. We observe the interplay of countless causal networks that make up our being – ever-changing streams of causality that, like evolution, are constantly flowing through us, forming and re-forming who we are and how we are in the world. The Buddha emphasises the importance of mindful meditation as a method of enquiry and realisation – a way of observing impermanence in process. He once summed up his teaching by saying to a group of students that if anyone from another sect should ask where the Buddha lived during the long rainy season, they should answer by saying: 'During the rains, friends, the Buddha generally dwelt in mindfulness of breathing.... it is a noble dwelling'.[1]

There are those who consider the practice of sitting meditation to be a self-centred and individualistic activity that only benefits the meditator. No doubt the most immediate effect of mindful meditation is experienced by the practitioner, however as we have seen, paradoxically, one of the main effects on the individual is to change both how the individual experiences himself, or herself, and to transform the way they relate to other beings and with the world. It is in this way that the practice of meditation is associated with the development of feelings of kinship and compassion. Given that the universe is interwoven with networks of cause-and-effect, all beings are interconnected and what is done to one affects all the others. In this way we are all related. There is kinship and fellowship between all beings - from a fly on the wall to a Queen in her palace. Within Buddhism this realisation of interconnectedness and interdependence is a key factor in the development of principles of social interaction, community and environmental awareness, denoted by the three words *karuṇā*, *mettā* and *ahimsa*.

Karuṇā, is usually translated as compassion, and our word, 'compassion' comes from a Latin root, *compati* (*com* - together + *pati* - to suffer). In other words, 'compassion' denotes a sense of 'fellow-feeling', of shared suffering, of empathy, and a feeling of care and kindness to those who suffer as we do. Compassion grows out of a deep feeling of connectedness, interdependence and a shared state of being. Compassion, like friendliness (metta) is grounded in non-attachment, a letting-go or letting-be, which arises from an understanding of how the world *is* – in all its transient, interwoven glory. Jack Kornfield, a well-known Buddhist teacher and social activist, makes a distinction between feelings grounded in attachment ('I love this person or this thing. I want to hold it and to keep it') - that grasp and hold and aim to possess for oneself - and feelings grounded in non-attachment that are open, appreciative and unconditional.

Mettā is a Pali word, derived from, *mitta* - 'friend'. It is most often translated as 'loving-kindness', but a more accurate rendition might be 'true friendliness'. The Buddha suggests that friendliness (mettā) 'is the emancipation of mind ... friendliness radiates, shines and illumines.' With friendliness we are warmed and we give warmth; we are lit and we light others. In the light of non-clinging friendliness we see others as relatives, treating them with respect, tolerance and warmth. We might also consider mettā as denoting kinship: a feeling of brotherhood and sisterhood with all beings – beings who share our conditions of existence, namely, impermanence and interdependence.

Ahimsa is a Sanskrit word meaning: 'not to cause injury through actions, words or thoughts'; and also 'non-violence'. If all beings (indeed all things) are interdependent and inter-acting, and in constant process, any action, however small, affects all things. If all things are interconnected and interdependent, then they cannot be separable in any absolute sense. Likewise, there can be no easy distinction between oneself and the universe. We are what we are because everything else is as it is. In a sense, we are also what we are not; we are the universe; the universe is us. It is this profound feeling of interdependence and interpenetration, and the empathy that arises from it, that leads us to want to care for other beings and for the world around us - for to injure or harm any part of the universe would be to harm both ourselves and our relatives.

Revision and reorientation – realising our interwoven nature

The process of mindful meditation, as described above, is a process of realisation – realising with dispassionate clarity how impermanence, interdependence and interpenetration are integral characteristics of existence. This realisation is accompanied by a change in the way the meditator relates to his or her experience – a space opens up in which experiences can be seen with great clarity without the layers of comment and judgment that are habitually added to a thought, feeling or sensation. We begin to see things as they are, without the burden of our habitual reactions to them. Our routine fixations and patterns of response are dissolved by non-reactive awareness. In this way we feel a lightening of experience and a letting-go of the clinging that tends to characterise our relationship to thoughts, feelings and the whole field of consciousness.

We also develop a new freedom of thought, feeling and action that is less acquisitive and self-centred, enabling us to relate to other beings and to our environment, without seeing them and it as alien objects ripe for possession and exploitation. This change can be seen as a shift towards a more ecological, balanced and less divisive worldview. To experience the world as interwoven with ourselves and with all beings, is to feel a kinship that might be the key to changing what we do in the world – to work towards alleviating the suffering of others and to establish a more sustainable presence on the earth.

---

[1] My re-working of a translation by Stephen Batchelor.

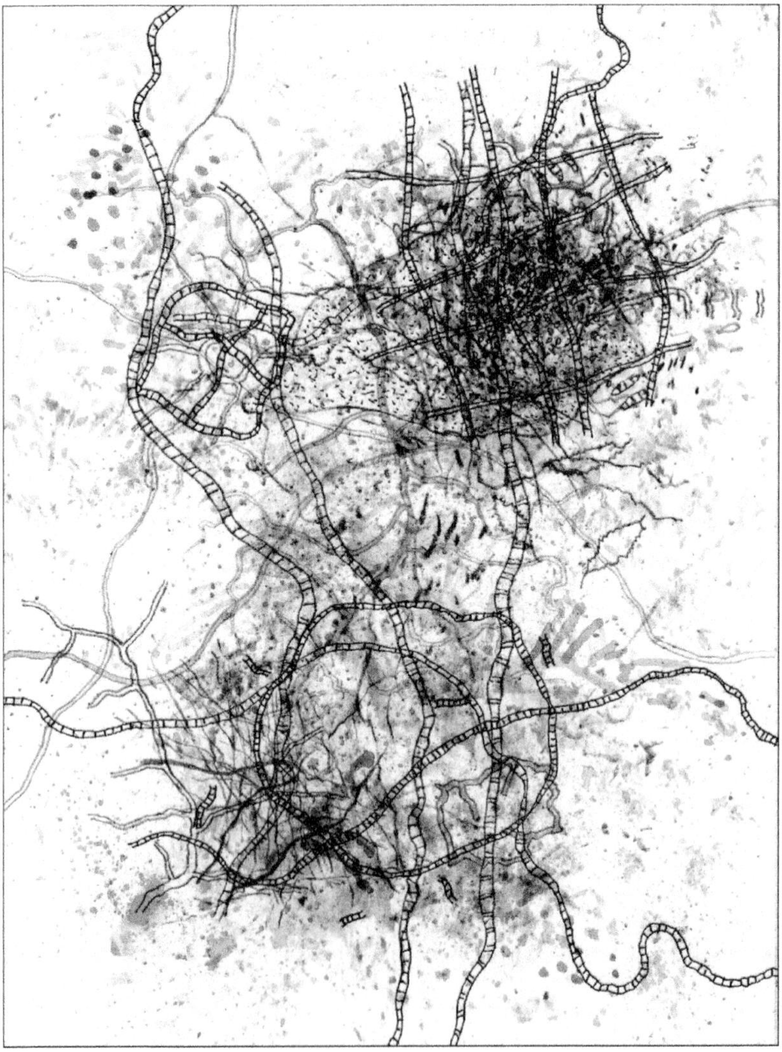

XV. THE OLD MAN SEES DEATH AS PART OF THE CONTINUUM OF LIFE

I have a small book and in it I write most days. For me it is an act of contemplation or prayer. It is also an act of elimination, defining a thing by ruling out all those things it can't be. But it is never as simple as that. This is the kind of foolishness I write: I am not this tree. I am not this stone. I am not this sky, or cloud, or blueness. I am not the shadow under the oak. I am not grass waving in a gentle breeze. I am not this or that, up or down, lost or found. Yet I am all of these things.

I am not mucous, spit, urine, blood, sperm, pus, tears, anger or sorrow. I am not feather, skin or scale. I am not grass, leaf, bark, stone or bone. I am not the singing bird or the dust on a pigeon's wing. I am not the immigrant sitting alone or the friend in a room full of friends. I am all of these things.

I am not the lost envelope or the found letter. I am not this toothache or that headache, or this blissful freedom from pain. I am not the billowing curtain or the shadow on the wall. I am not the tree that sings or the sea of despair. I am not all the things on this table or the table or the things that have fallen to the floor or the floor or the dust on the floor. I am not him or her or it or perhaps or maybe or might or will or has or shall or can or never or always. I am not today or tomorrow or yesterday. I am not one pebble on a shore of pebbles. I am not one book in the libraries of the world and I am not the libraries or the world. I am not the writer of this list, nor am I the list, or the ink, or the pen that writes, or the arm that holds the pen that writes, or the writing. I am not red or yellow or blue or black or green or grey or brown or white or light or dark or absence of any of these. I am not now or ever or forever. I am all of these things.

I am not the letter H or J or T or D or any other letter in any alphabet, or any word or sentence or paragraph written or spoken or sung. I am not what I am not nor what I am. I am not the body that casts this shadow or the shadow cast. I am not the apparition in the mirror or the glass or the light that meets the glass. I am not the tramp curled up in the doorway or the man entering the doorway or the man who holds open the door. I am not nor am I. I am all of these things.

It is a kind of nonsense to write in this way, a fumbling in the dark, nudging against the edges of things but unable to define what they are. In a sense things are only the edges, the fragmentary sensations that infuse our embodied minds. To search for definitions or essences is the real foolishness, for there are none, only the passing flood of impressions, sights, sounds.....

We are both the sweeper and the swept, the broom moving across the floor and the dust that rises and falls.

> *as the apples fall*
> *as if returning*
> *to foetus sleep*
> *in a churned*
> *womb of leaf-mash*
> *and stubbled grass*
>
> *so it is in Autumn*
> *when the tarmac*
> *glistens with skins*
> *of berry and worm*
> *and disgorged snails*
>
> *an arrow of geese*
> *syringes the air*
> *and cuts a ditch*
> *towards estuarine*
> *watermeadows*
>
> *some days there is just*
> *too much to reckon with*
> *too grave a toll of tales*
> *passing into history's*
> *bucket*

The old man sees death as part of the continuum of life 171

yet we are here and breathe
this mossy air with all our senses
bursting – so much starlight
on the tongue that it is hard
to say where we end and the rest
begins

A few nights ago I dreamt I was a beam of sunlight heading toward the blue globe of the earth. As I got closer I could see the ocean and the green land and also I could see the rainbow hues of all the creatures living on land and in the seas. They

hummed and called and spoke and sang with every imaginable sound and melody. They moved in every possible fashion: walking, slithering, crawling, sliding, swooping, gliding, flapping, swimming, climbing, diving....... They manifested the most improbable shapes, from simple to complex, mundane to fantastic. And they radiated energy, power, inventiveness and life. As well as those I could see and hear, I sensed all the invisible beings, too small to see, or hidden inside other beings, or within the mineral realms of mountain and desert. And they were just as dynamic, sensing in their turn the codes of other lives, pulses of their hosts and companions. And it was beautiful and wondrous to see such wealth, such profligacy of form, sound, taste and smell. There was nothing I could dream or conceive that wasn't already somewhere on that blue sphere, meeting my eyes, tongue, ears, nose and skin. It was as if some force had made even a single cell have within it the power and creativity to give forth unlimited variety and diversity – generating a stream of every possible way of living. And here it was, on this earth, like a radiant sun itself, showering my senses with its playful excess, abandon and plurality.

As I awoke from such vibrant dreaming, I became once more the sunbeam of my own living span, sensing around me the exuberant plenitude of life in all its forms. At each daybreak and each sundown I look around and give thanks for sunlight and all the creative chemistry of life and am reminded that it is this living interwoven beauty of planet earth that is our special gift to the universe.

As my time grows nearer I think of death and what it is and what it means. I know for Christians, Muslims, Jews and many others, there is the prospect of an afterlife, a place beyond this earthly domain in which individuals will recognise themselves in a rejuvenated form and meet with those they have known who have already entered the kingdom of glory. I find it hard to understand this idea. It seems to me there are too many anomalies: if we meet again with those who have died presumably we meet not only our friends and those we love and admire, but also our enemies and those we have no time for – this hardly makes for a time of serenity and everlasting peace. Why is there so little evidence to support this belief in a life after death? And why should we believe this particular unverifiable idea when we discount most other ideas that have no proof? And what of the population question? If we seem to be packed cheek by jowl here on earth, what is it like in heaven? And if in heaven we have no bodies how do we feel serenity or pleasure or everlasting peace? And if peace is everlasting is it peace at all, given that peace only makes sense in relation to war or disturbance or conflict? Peace for ever would seem like an interminable steady state, and an unchanging state of any kind would lose its particular flavour quite quickly and we would sink into a kind of oblivion where nothing happened because anything happening always has the potential to disturb or excite, sending ripples of uncertainty through the predictable serenity of heaven.... No it all seems too routine, too determinedly even, unsurprising and lacking in life!

For me there is heaven all around. Every day brings something new, something surprising, something that makes me think and ponder and wonder. I have a body and it is a body full of windows and doors through which I can sense this world overflowing with sights and sounds, touches, odours and tastes. Every pore in my skin is a point of contact, an opening through which energies flow in and out. I am host to a myriad of creatures, on either side of my skin, enriching, cleaning, maintaining and, at times, threatening, my life. They are my closest relatives, always at hand, companions on the road of life. I exist with them. They are part of me, and I them. We co-inhabit this nomadic territory I call my body. They come and go, as do I, cell by cell, in cycles of growth and decay, throughout

the days and years of what I mistakenly refer to as 'my' life – for it is their life as much as mine.

Every day that dawns is a kind of resurrection, a small renaissance, a stepping into fresh pastures. Even though I have lived here for many years, each day I get out of bed in a slightly different way and each step I take from then on is never the same as the day before. Although there is an aura of familiarity, there is also a glow of surprise and change. And just as new pleasures come with things noticed for the first time, so I feel aches and pains that I have not felt before. The body is always changing, a site of transformation and uncertainty. As I get older my limbs stiffen, joints move less fluently, muscles are capable of less work than they once managed. This is how it is and how it will continue until some gaggle of bacteria or viruses, or clumsy fall, or failure of heart or mind, will bring the whole community of my being to an apparent end.

Yet, of course, the living systems continue, cells begin to break down, bacteria and other microbes take on new jobs, organisms move in to devour and digest what has become a transitional being, a state of decay that is also a state of renewal and re-emergence. On the other hand, it may be a burning, a more rapid transition from flesh to smoke and ash. Even so, the chemicals will be re-shuffled and dispersed, and atoms will be returned to the cosmic store to be used again and again. In this sense there will be a recycling, a returning, a moving on to some other state. Not heaven perhaps, and not a continuation of this particular congregation of parts that constitutes this particular old man, but a continuation nonetheless, a chemical migration that is just as surprising and marvellous. And who knows what form these newly released atoms might take in ages to come. Perhaps this is re-incarnation and re-birth, another dance of the playful cosmic forces that engender life after life, and life within life.

I am content that this is how it is, or how I see it. I like the idea that my bundle of aggregates gets re-distributed and re-formed into new structures of being. Somehow there is something re-assuring about the idea that the community that makes up this old man eventually disbands, like a clan of nomads who get together for the winter, only to separate into smaller groups to spend the summer in different places. The community which makes up my bundle of flesh, bones and brain has been together off and on for a lifetime, but then its constituent atoms, cells and organisms are reshuffled and dispersed, finding new places to rest, new companions to spend time with, new sensations and narratives to give voice to.

We are all wanderers – 'dusty feet', as travelling merchants were called in medieval times – en route to who-knows-where, passers-by, shape-shifting hoboes without a fixed abode yet at home everywhere.

I seem to remember a line by the Zen teacher, Bassui, writing to a disciple who was dying:

> *Your end, which is endless,*
> *is as a snowflake dissolving*
> *in pure air* [1]

Seen from a perspective of earthly transformation and the shrinking of glaciers, I think of it like this:

> *For century after century*
> *the ice thickened and spread*
> *and returned light to the*
> *sky*
>
> *... in a few decades*
> *it will be gone*
>
> *the lives*
> *of ice and men:*
>
> *a thickening*
> *and a melting...*

---

[1] This is probably Bassui Tokushō (1327-1387), a teacher in the Rinzai school of Japanese Zen Buddhism.

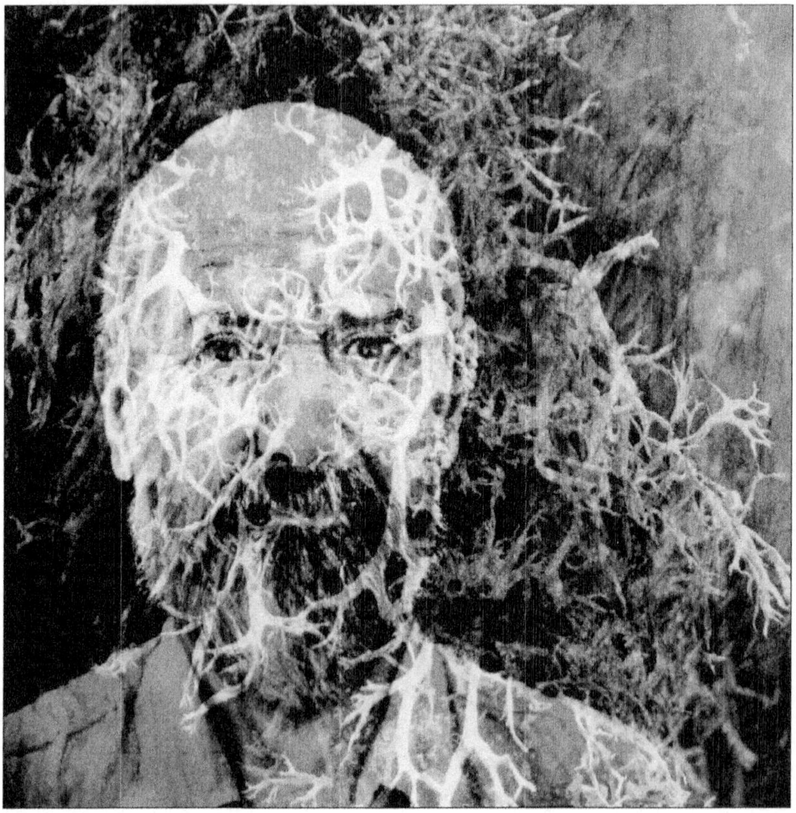

CODA

It could be argued that we all have an old and young person within us, and that these two voices are intertwined in the stories we tell, the beliefs we hold and the opinions we have about ourselves and the world. As our days come and go we spin and weave together memories, images, ideas and beliefs that enable us to make sense of our existence and to deal with the situations that arise from day to day. There are many threads to this weaving and though there may be a fluid coherence to what we weave, there may also be many inconsistencies, tangles and frayed edges. These anomalies are traces of our coping with the contradictions and surprises that confront us from moment to moment. Living is not, for most people, a process of seamless harmony and consistency – it is often a complex and messy business, replete with wrong turnings, half-finished projects, unexpected dead ends and unfathomable mysteries. We never know what the next day or season has in store for us, and we have to be resourceful, adaptive and attentive if we are to handle the stream of puzzles, problems and stresses that our engagement in the world engenders.

Even if we try, we cannot cut ourselves off from the context in which we live, indeed, in a sense, we *are* that context - we are interactive, interdependent beings, always renewing, revising and recreating ourselves as our experience unfolds. And our experiences are of the world as much as of us, just as our skin is as much the skin of the world. We are porous embodied minds through which flow the sensations, feelings and thoughts that constitute our experience, and those sensations, thoughts and feelings are of a world that is transmuted into *our* world.

*

Multifarious forms of life inhabit every nook and cranny of the surface of planet earth – from the benign regions of forest and prairie, to the most inhospitable areas of baked desert and polar ice.

Organisms live at the bottom of the deepest ocean canyons and in the sulphurous acidic geysers that spew out of the earth's core. Many micro-organisms live within larger ones, functioning as part of a greater whole while retaining their own distinctive form. We benefit from the bacteria in our digestive system and the bacteria benefit from us as a hospitable host. Between us we maintain a mutual existence that is balanced and conducive to the wellbeing of both of us. Indeed this relationship is so effective and fundamental to our existence that the use of 'ours' and 'we', is more appropriate than 'mine' and 'me'.

We are only now coming to understand that all the diverse forms of life, from the smallest and simplest, to the largest and most complex, interact within networks of mutuality and cooperation. They respond to the environment, and to each other, with sensitivity and reciprocity. They sense their habitats of earth, water and air in ways that are often baffling to us – sensitive to parts of the electro-magnetic spectrum that lie outside the narrow range we experience. Honey bees, salamanders and some species of migrating birds sense changes in the earth's magnetic field to find their way around; some species of snake sense infra-red light; leeches have a highly developed tactile receptivity to temperature and chemical compounds, enabling them to find a suitable patch of skin to puncture and draw blood; bees, butterflies and reindeer perceive ultra-violet light; sharks and rays are able to emit and perceive electrical pulses through electro-receptors in their muscles; bats and some marine mammals use echo-location to sense their environment – effectively 'seeing' with sound; dogs, meerkats and wolverines have a highly developed sense of smell, way beyond the range of humans. Taken together with the various kinds of receptors found in plants, this evidence suggests that the whole biosphere senses, and makes sense of, a significant proportion of the electro-magnetic spectrum, and we can consider the earth as having a sentient dimension.

*

Many, possibly most, organisms, (including plants, animals and humans) exchange information through a diverse array of codes, signs and languages. Audible, tactile, visual and chemical modes of communication are used to signal to each other in ways that we are only now beginning to understand. Sensing and communing seem to be inextricably linked in communication systems that weave together all the beings that inhabit the earth. Trees, bacteria, locusts and humans hum with energy and information. They constitute small currents of communication and sensing within the vast vibrant field of voices and perceptions that envelop our planet. Indeed, the earth's surface can be said to be sentient *and* communicative – buzzing with information and sensory exchange – a dynamic array of receptors and transmitters woven together into a functioning system that is alive and alert, attending to itself, to its parts and to its cosmic context. We could consider this as the original 'world wide web', the sentient internet of the biosphere. We are all kindred beings within this great web of sensation, sign and song. It is this animate, polyphonic and polymorphic world that we inhabit and to which we contribution.

The diversity of sensory and information-processing systems across species of plants and animals gives rise to a similar diversity of cultures. From lichens to eagles, pine trees to ants, sea cucumbers to humans, all organisms have distinctive patterns of behaviour, sensory input and communication – they have distinctive cultures, and these cultures are interactive with, and interdependent upon, each other. Each culture has an evolutionary history, shaped by responses to, and interaction with, its ever-changing habitat. Each culture is comprised of an array of signs, codes and behaviours that together form a collective memory and worldview. Each community of organisms has its own stories, songs, images and constructions – manifested in chemical, auditory, visual, spatial or other modes. Taken together, this interwoven tapestry of diverse languages and forms echoes the diversity of sensory interactions between organisms and their environment.

*

In the European culture of my immediate family of humans, the complex interwoven compositions of Bach or Vivaldi, can be considered as emblematic analogues of the sentient, information-processing networks that clothe our world. Perhaps it is that we can hear these structural echoes in the canons and fugues that form and dissolve in Bach's work, or in the endless variations of melodic line and rhythm that give shape and dynamism to Vivaldi's creations. And these interwoven compositions have similarities to the intricate visual structures developed by Celtic peoples living in different parts of Europe between 400 BCE and medieval times. These sinuous organic forms have a dense but fluid character that is reminiscent of bramble hedges, ivy and watery currents.

In the iconic 'insular' illuminated manuscripts that were produced between c.650-1200 CE in Lindisfarne, Durham, Ireland, and in other monastic communities across Europe, lines snake around each other giving shape to highly stylised plants and animals, and to individual letters or words. These are just a few examples of European cultural forms that echo the sentient world wide web of the biosphere.

Other examples can be found in many cultures of the extended human family across the globe, for instance: the complex stylizations of the Haida peoples in North Western North America; the subtle scales and rhythmic patterns in the *ragas* of Indian classical music; the 'dot' paintings of some Australian native peoples; the complex geometric patterns in Islamic art and architecture; and, Polynesian art and body adornment. All of these visual and auditory modes of art can be considered as emblematic of the sensory and communicative biosphere, of the intermingling of minds, and of the interwoven nature of all living beings.

BIBLIOGRAPHY

Abram, David. 1997. The Spell of the Sensuous. New York: Vintage Books.
Anon. 2000. Concise Routledge Encyclopedia of Philosophy. London: Routledge
Anon. 2002. Shorter Oxford English Dictionary. Oxford: Oxford University Press.
Anson, P.F. 1964. The Call of the Desert. London: S.P.C.K.
Baker, B. & Henry, G. eds. 1999. Merton and Sufism: The Untold Story – A Complete Compendium. Louisville Kentucky: Fons Vitae.
Barrett, William. 1990. Irrational Man: A Study in Existential Philosophy. New York: Anchor Books.
Batchelor, Stephen. 2010. Confession of a Buddhist Atheist. New York: Spiegel & Grau.
Basho. (Yuasa, Nobuyuki, trans.). 1966. The Narrow Road to the Deep North and Other Travel Sketches. Harmondsworth, UK: Penguin.
Blair, Michelle, trans. 2004. The Wanderer. Online at: http://homepages.bw.edu/~uncover/blairtranslation.htm (consulted 21/08/2016).
Blaser, Robin, ed. 1975. The Collected Books of Jack Spicer. Los Angeles, USA: Black Sparrow Press.
Blyth, R.H. 1949. Haiku Volume 1: Eastern Culture. Tokyo: The Hokuseido Press.
Borges, Jorge Luis. 1973. An Introduction to American Literature. New York: Schocken Books.
Borges, Jorge Luis. 1985. Jorge Luis Borges: Selected Poems 1923-1967. London: Penguin.
Bragg, Melvyn. 2003. The Adventure of English: The Biography of a Language. London: Hodder & Stoughton.

Briscoe, Robert, trans. Undated. *The Seafarer*, in Goodwin, Arthur. Undated. Translations from the Exeter Book: Selections of Anglo-Saxon Poetry. Exeter: Exeter College of Art.

Bryson, B. 2004. A Short History of Nearly Everything. London: Black Swan

Bullock, A. & Trombley, S. eds. 2000. The New Fontana Dictionary of Modern Thought. London: Harper Collins.

Capra, Fritjof. 1990. The Turning Point. London: Fontana.

Carson, Anne. 2003. If Not Winter: Fragments of Sappho. London: Virago.

Clark, Andy & Chalmers, David J. 1998. The Extended Mind. Online at: http://cogprints.org/320/1/extended.html (consulted 17/12/2015).

Colegate, Isabel. 2002. A Pelican in the Wilderness: hermits, solitaries and recluses. London: Harper Collins.

Connor, Steve. 2009. How the human skin is a des res for bacteria, The Independent, 29 May 2009.

Cummings, E.E. 1963. e.e.cummings: selected poems 1923-1958. London: Penguin.

Danvers, J. 2006. Picturing Mind: Paradox, Indeterminacy and Consciousness in Art & Poetry. Amsterdam & New York: Rodopi.

Davenport, Guy. 1984. The Geography of the Imagination. London: Pan Books.

Davenport, Guy. 2003. The death of Picasso: new & selected writings. Washington, DC: Shoemaker & Hoard.

Davidson, Keir. 2007. A Zen Life in Nature: Musō Soseki in his Gardens. Ann Arbor, USA: Center for Japanese Studies, University of Michigan.

Dreyfus, Georges, B.J. 2003. The Sound of Two Hands Clapping: The Education of a Tibetan Buddhist Monk. Berkeley & Los Angeles: University of California Press.

Duncan, Robert. 1968. The First Decade: Selected Poems 1940-1950. London: Fulcrum Press.

Durr, R.A. 1962. On the Mystical Poetry of Henry Vaughan. Cambridge, Massachusetts: Harvard University Press.

Eco, U. 2002. Art and Beauty in the Middle Ages. New Haven USA: Yale University Press.

Printed in Great Britain
by Amazon